DISCOVER THE
Game Alias®
with

Alias | Learning Tools

ACKNOWLEDGEMENTS

Cover & book design:
Louis Fishauf, Ian McFadyen

Cover image:
Petre Gheorghian

Production designers
Mike Barker, Diane Erlich

Contributing authors:
Rob Ormond, Marc Beaudoin

Editorial services:
Erica Fyvie

Additional technical review:
David Lau, Curtis Garton

DVD production:
Roark Andrade, Julio Lopez

Production Coordinator:
Lenni Rodrigues

Project Manager:
Carla Sharkey

Product Manager, Learning Tools and Training:
Danielle Lamothe

Director, Learning Tools and Training:
Michael Stamler

A special thanks goes out to:
Carmela Bourassa, May Chiu, James Christopher, Deion Green, Rachael Jackson,
Lorraine McAlpine, Brahm Nathans, Robert Lin and Yojiro Nishimura

We would like to thank Red Eye Studio (www.red-eyestudio.com) for providing the
bonus materials included in this book's DVD-ROM.

⊙Alias | Learning Tools

ABOUT THE AUTHORS

Primary Author, Japanese Edition

Katsunori Kondo | Designer Bank Corporation

Katsunori Kondo is President of the Designer Bank Corporation and has an extensive background in the Games industry. Formerly a 3D CG Designer with SNK Corporation and Polygon Magic, Inc. Kondo-san felt that there was a lack of resources for artists working within his industry. This book was motivated by his desire to share his hard-learned secrets with others in the games industry and with those aspiring to join it.

Contributing Authors, Japanese Edition

Yumiko Sugihara, Hideki Shiroma, Go Takeshi

Contributing Authors, English Edition

Rob Ormond | Alias

Rob Ormond has worked for Alias since 1999 and is based in the Toronto office. He is a Senior Support Engineer, an Alias certified instructor and has also provided consulting services to a wide variety of Alias customers. Rob's areas of specialization include the games industry, animation, and workflow development. Rob has presented Maya MasterClasses™ at Siggraph and the Games Developer's Conference on topics such as Polygonal Lighting and Texturing and Shading.

Marc Beaudoin | Alias

Marc Beaudoin is an Alias MotionBuilder Product Specialist working in the Alias Montréal office. In November 2000, Marc joined Kaydara (acquired by Alias in 2004) where he has provided technical director consultancy services on a wide variety of projects using Motion Capture and Alias MotionBuilder. In addition to his extensive MotionBuilder knowledge, Marc is also a Maya certified instructor with a focus on Character Animation, MEL™ scripting and Dynamics. Marc was a Power Animator/Maya instructor at the Université de Québec à Montréal from 1996-2000. In recent years, Marc has also conducted custom training courses in a wide variety of studios around the world including Sony Images Works, ID software, DreamQuest Studio, UbiSoft and Vox Populi.

Red Eye Studio is a motion capture, animation and effects facility located in Hoffmann Estates, Illinois, just outside of Chicago. Red Eye's state-of-the-art performance capture studio is designed to fulfill the needs of any production, whether it be film, television, video games, sports analysis, medical research, or educational development.

ABOUT THIS BOOK

Thank you for choosing *Discover the Game with Alias*. This book is intended to provide the intermediate 3D software user with an overview of the techniques and workflows recommended when creating models and animations for games. *Discover the Game with Alias* is based on working in two of the industry's standard applications: Maya and Alias MotionBuilder. However, the techniques explored here are sound regardless of your software of choice. In order to use this book, you should have:

- Maya Complete 7, Maya Unlimited 7, or Maya Personal Learning Edition 7

- Alias MotionBuilder 7, or Alias MotionBuilder Personal Learning Edition 7

- DVD-ROM Drive

DVD-ROM

The DVD-ROM at the back of this book contains several resources to accelerate your learning experience including:

- Fully-rigged character

- Instructor-led movies

- Props used throughout the book

- Support files

- Library of 24 Motion Capture moves and tutorial from Red Eye Studio

Because learning never stops, we've included 24 Motion Capture moves (US $600.00 value) for your use provided by Red Eye Studio. In addition, Red Eye Studio has generously included a tutorial on importing and applying the moves to a skeleton. To access these files, copy the *Red_Eye_Studio* folder from the DVD-ROM at the back of this book to your computer.

Find out more about Red Eye Studio at www.redeye-studio.com.

Installing support files – before beginning the lessons in this book, you will need to install the lesson support files. Copy the project directories found in the *support_files* folder on the accompanying DVD-ROM onto your computer.

Updates to This Book

In an effort to ensure your continued success through the lessons in this book, please visit our web site for the latest updates available: *www.alias.com/learningtools_updates/*

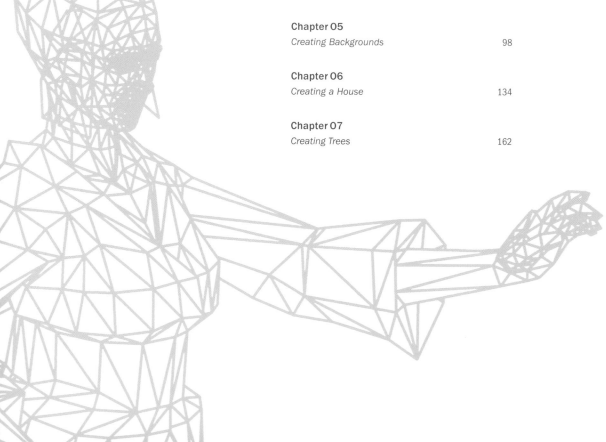

Section **Four**   Alias MotionBuilder

Chapter 01

BACKGROUND INFORMATION

Background Information

We will begin by examining the basics of game production with a focus mainly on the game outline and game specifications. We will be working in Maya to create a character and basic game level.

• Teams in the Game Production Pipeline

It involves a great deal of teamwork to create releases for game consoles or the personal computer. Usually, the teams are divided into four categories: game planners, game programmers, game audio designers and game designers.

• The Game Planner

A game planner's role is devising the game itself. A game planner oversees areas such as the general game structure, the concept and the story. These areas will greatly affect the overall "appeal" of the game.

Commonly, many game outlines are more than a hundred pages. A lot of brainpower is involved in devising these various ideas. Game planners often keep a notepad with them day and night so that they can record anything that springs to mind.

A game planner will coordinate resources with all teams. The role may be best suited for individuals that are comfortable with and capable of managing others. This book is about creating and designing assets for games including modeling, rigging and texturing models in Maya.

• The Game Programmer

A game programmer's role is to code a game. They are responsible for game fundamentals such as how a screen reacts when the user presses a particular button, how to display many characters without slowing down a game, etc. With the current game consoles, i.e. PlayStation 2® , Xbox® or GameCube® , the possibilities of game interaction and the level of detail have increased dramatically, depending on the game programmer's level of skill. This evolution in potential will continue with the development of next generation platforms, such as Xbox® 360.

• The Game Audio Designer

Game audio designers are responsible for the soundtrack and sound effects of a game. This last stage of the process can greatly enhance the excitement in a game.

One

The Game Designer

Most of the readers will presumably fall under this category. If we further breakdown the roles of a game designer, they are 2D designer, modeler and CG animator.

A 2D designer draws expressive illustrations, taken from a game planner's images, text descriptions, or roughly drawn sketches. A 2D designer also imagines interesting characters and background designs. Based on the 2D designer's work, a modeler transfers an expression in the 2D world into the 3D world, adding the modeler's own sensibilities. A CG animator adds movement to game characters.

The Game Outline

In CG game production, you have what are called game outlines and game specifications. When creating a game, a game designer must read the game outline first for an overall idea of the game and its concepts. Furthermore, it is necessary for a game designer to also check the game specifications for the polygon count, number of texture layers, proper and improper rules, etc.

What is a Game Outline?

In the outline, a game planner devises and summarizes the scenario, character concepts, historical time period, background setting, game operability, etc. The following is an example of a game outline:

Game Title: *Geisha Wars*

Genre: Action adventure

Scenario: Centered on the character Miyako, *Geisha Wars* is a Japanese-style fantasy, with gods inhabiting things in the natural world through their spells and spirits.

Time Period: Late 16th century feudal Japan

Platform: PlayStation 3

Sales Strategy: With the revival of samurai related Japanese stories, the game will be released overseas as well.

Game outline

An integral part of the game outline is the game background or layout. A game background is a rough top or side view diagram depicting a layout like a map. Symbols like circles and squares are used as identifying markers so that other team members will know what major landmarks are in the game. This part of the game outline also provides the game save points, item locations and road connections.

A 2D game designer color illustrates the artwork for the game based on the game planner's more abstract drawings.

Once a 2D game designer's illustrations are approved by the game planner, a 3D game designer finally transfers the 2D illustrations into 3D models.

As an important first step, primitive 3D CG models are created without polygon restrictions. These primitive models are shown on screen to check for traits unforeseen in the 2D illustration. Unexpected problems may include: a model looking different from the one conceived in 2D, a road in the map layout being too narrow once placed in a 3D setting, or an object being larger than initially conceived. In this book, when we model the character, buildings and environment, we will be using many tips and tricks to bring the poly count down.

Once the primitive model looks satisfactory, it is time to start improving upon it.

• 3D CG Game Production Pipeline

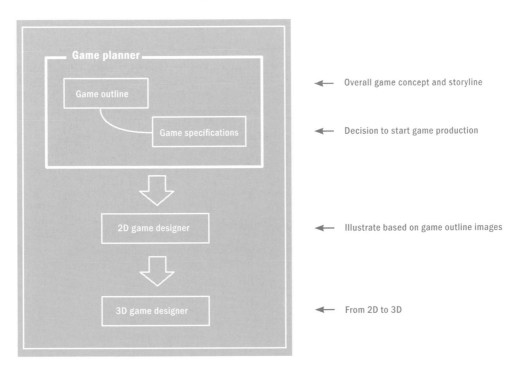

• Game Specifications

Vital rules for the game production are outlined in the game specifications.

ITEMS IN THE GAME SPECIFICATIONS

Software: Depending on the work, the CG production software varies considerably. Maya, Photoshop, C++ programing environment.

Polygon Count: The overall number of allowed polygons. Before modeling, people often plan where and how many polygons to use.

Polygon Size: If a polygon size is too large, when the camera zooms-in a polygon may appear fragmented. For such cases, the size of any one polygon may be restricted.

Texture Size: Size of any one texture (height x width). Always draw textures that fit the texture size.

Texture Measurement: The number of pixels in a texture equalling one meter in the real world - the proposed standard in determining texture measurement.

Alpha Priority: Overlapping textured models with alpha channels may appear odd on-screen. The Alpha Priority consists of rules to cope with this problem.

Object Arrangement: Specifies whether instancing can be used. Depending on whether or not it can be used, the modeling methods change a great deal.

Height of Stairs, etc: If a model's height exceeds a certain amount, it cannot be climbed.

• Example Game Outline and Game Specifications

Keeping the preceding points in mind, let us now look at the game outline and game specifications of a sample game production.

Changes often occur in the midst of game production in areas such as character costume design. When that happens, the changes may create a lot of problems. Depending on the game production company, the modelers, texture painters and animators may be on separate teams. The following specifications were made with a PlayStation game development in mind.

CHARACTER DESIGN OUTLINE

Height: 180 centimeters, includes elevated hair, 170 centimeters excluding hair.

Weight: 55 kilograms

Dominate Hand: Right-handed

Weapon: Prefers the katana sword 'Kokorone'

Age: 28 (estimate)

Characteristics: A stoic, monk-like image. Clothes do not expose too much of the upper body and they allow easy movement. The character has the cold, indifferent mood of a European model.

NO 01 - Miyako - c01-00

Software: Maya 7.0

File Name: *ch_001.mb*

Polygon Count: Under 2500 polygons

Texture Resolution: 512x256 pixels, 1 layer or less

Color Resolution: 256 color

Texture File: Names, Color channel only *c001_01_NAME.bmp 1-bit Alpha, c001_02_NAME.tga, 8-bit Alpha: c001_03_NAME.tga*

Object File Names: Normal, no restrictions

Work Time: 20 days

Overall Work Pipeline: 20 days, listed below

Modeling: 5 days, Weighting (includes movement adjustments) - 5 days

Texturing: 5 days, overall adjustments – 5 days

- **Outline of Game Background**

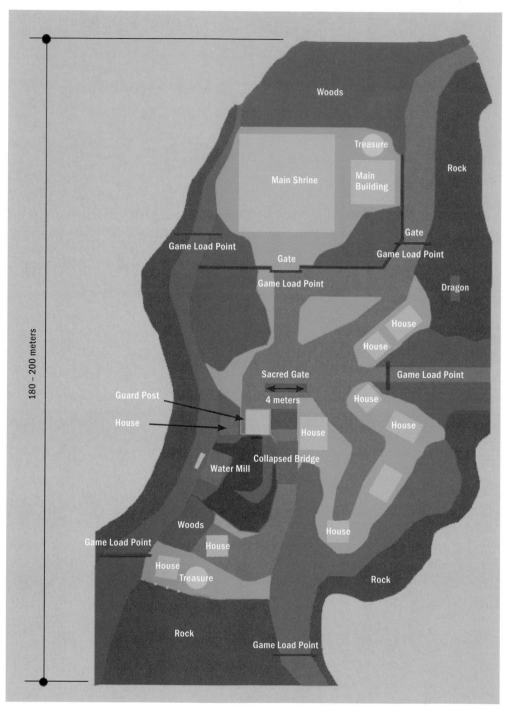

Game Planner's Map Layout

Map Illustrations by 2D Illustrators

Enemy Characters/Triggered Game Events/Accessible Buildings

Stage Boss: Two-headed dragon (Main Shrine)

Basic Enemy Characters: Giant toads (in and around the river), wolves (throughout map), forest spirits (around the woods) and two-headed dogs (around shrine compound).

Items: Life potions / Special Item: entwined scroll

Triggered Game Events: Talking to the water mill guard triggers a quest to find the entwined scroll. It is behind a hidden door, on the top floor of the main building. Pushing a decorative suit of armor reveals the hidden door.

Accessible Buildings: Shrine buildings, guard post and water aill (game loads when accessing each building).

● Game Background Specifications Outline

NO 01 - Yugen no sato - m01-00

Software: Maya 7.0

File Name: *map_001.mb*

Polygon Count: Maximum 20,000 polygons for one map

Polygon Size: Maximum size when the camera zooms-in is 5 x 5 meters.

Texture Resolution: (For 256 color) About 20 sheets of 256 x 256 pixels each.

Texture Size: 8 x 8, 16 x 16, 32 x 32, 64 x 64, 128 x 128, 256 x 256 pixels. Generally, 256 x 256 pixel sheets.

Texture Measurement: 1 meter squared equals 64 x 64 pixels.

Texture File Names: Color channel only, *m001_01_NAME.bmp*, 1-bit Alpha, *m001_02_NAME.tga*, 8-bit Alpha, *m001_03_NAME.tga*

Object File Names:

Normal - No restrictions, Instance (Object Arrangement), NAME_001, NAME_002,

Backgrounds - mo_NAME_a, mo_NAME_b,

Sky - sky_NAME,

Clouds - cl_NAME_a, cl_NAME_b

Alpha Priority: From above the node, display in order (ordering begins with objects farthest away from the camera).

Other Polygon Specifications: Dual-sided, square polygons allowed. No more than five lights per one polygon allowed.

Other Texture Specifications: Maximum two tilings for each UV.

Object Arrangement: Using Instance, set an original model's XYZ coordinates as (0, 0, 0).

Height of Stairs, etc.:

Stairs - height 25 x depth 50 centimeters

Height of Climbable Landscape - Maximum 25 centimeters

Slopes: Under 50 degrees

Work Time: 30 days

Overall Work Pipeline: 30 days, listed below
- **Modeling:** 10 days
- **Texture:** 10 days
- **Illumination:** 4 days
- **Overall Adjustments:** 6 days

> **Note:** *Often, a game planner's actual map layout may not be as detailed as the previous example. It may even be a crudely drawn map layout on graph paper, showing where everything is located. In principle, such a crude map is not a problem, so long as the locations of objects can be pointed out and identified. A 2D designer's illustrations are based on the game planner's layout.*

● Summary

In this chapter we briefly touched upon the minimum requirements for creating characters and backgrounds. After reviewing each individual step of game production, what may have initially seemed overwhelming will hopefully be clearer to you now.

In the next chapter we will examine how real-life CG professionals, at the forefront of the industry, create their models in Maya.

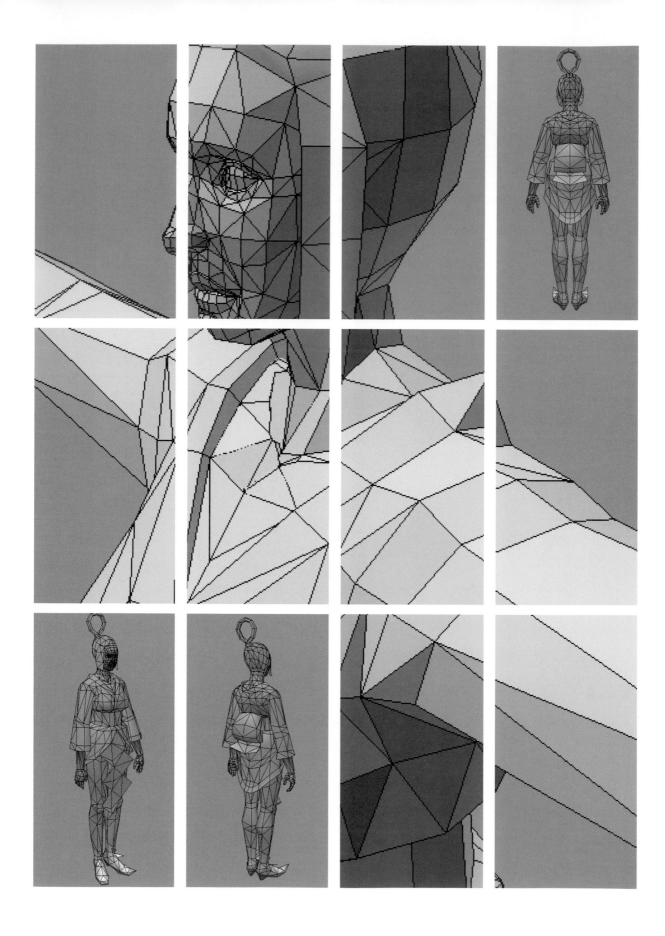

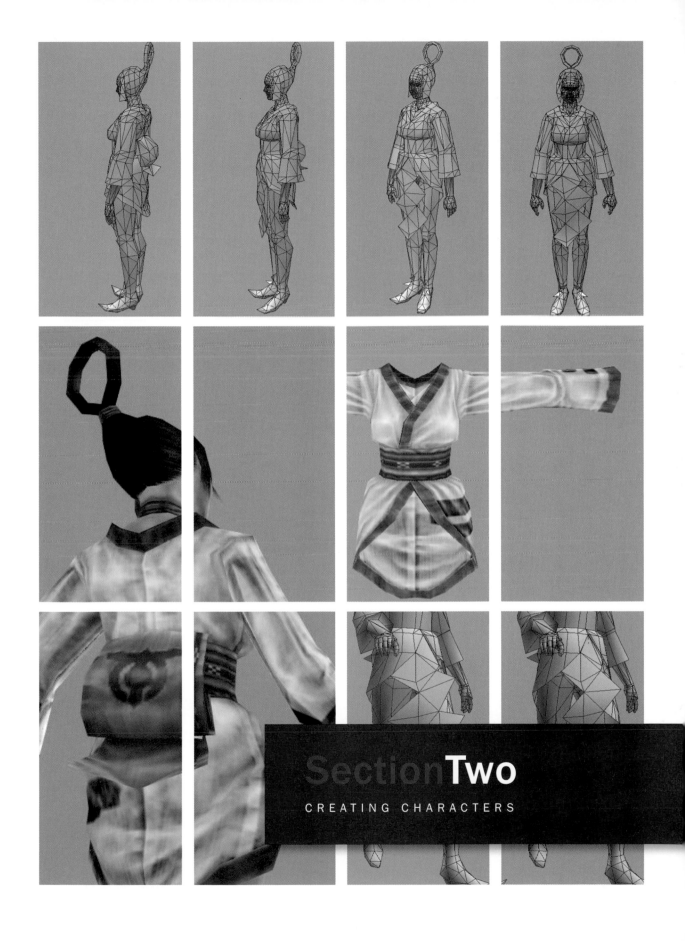

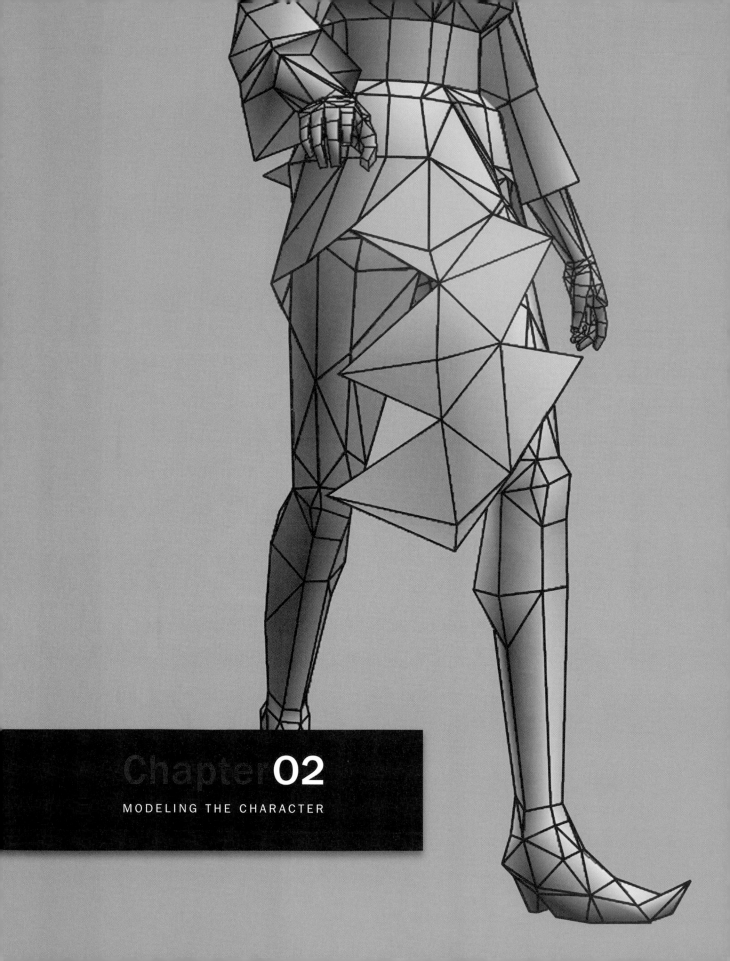

Chapter **02**

MODELING THE CHARACTER

Introduction

In character creation, with this realistic human design as an example, the fundamental body structure does not differ from conventional human anatomy. The same is true with a cartoon-style human design. Therefore, an understanding of human muscles and skeleton becomes important. As to how convincing the model itself looks, will depend on your knowledge of human anatomy.

A game character has a role in a specific game world; there are protagonists, secondary characters, monsters, villains and enemy bosses. Depending on the game character's role and personality, the appearance, body proportions and texture colors can change. Let us begin modeling the lead character.

● Character Creation Pipeline

We begin this process of modeling without skinning & skeleton creation, although that will vary with the project or game character.

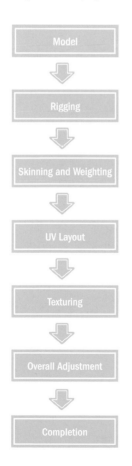

• Primitive Character Model

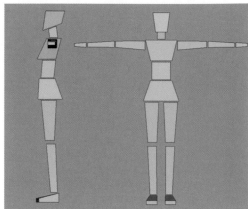

1. In order to get a sense of the proportions and articulation of the character, a simple version should be modeled using polygon cube primitives.

2. Using **Translate**, **Rotate** and **Scale Tools**, adjust the polygon cube shapes to approximate the character form. This stage is done without worrying too much about detail.

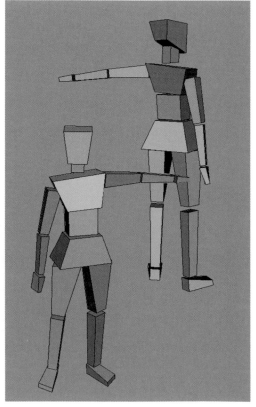

3. The rough character can be created with a basic skeleton. Skin the geometry to the appropriate joints. In doing so, the proportions can be easily assessed.

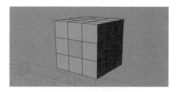

• Modeling The Face

1. After completing a rough model primitive to base our higher resolution model on, we can improve one body part at a time. Select all the body cubes and template (**Display** → **Object Display** → **Template**) the geometry in order to make the process of modeling easier to visualize.

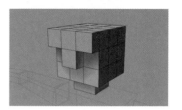

Let us begin by improving the body parts above the neck.

First, follow the diagram to the right to create a cube with appropriate dimensions for a head. Using **Edit Polygons** → **Extrude Face**, create additional detail for the neck, eyes and nose.

2. Leaving the present polygon count unchanged, translate vertices to round the head.

Where the shape may distort, add edges using **Edit Polygons** → **Split Polygon**.

Once able to see the general shape, we delete half the face.

In reality, a face or a body is technically not perfectly symmetrical. However, we will be modeling a symmetrical character. Therefore, we only need to model one side of the face or body, and then later mirror the part over to the other side.

> **Note:** *Within the Translate Tools' options, symmetry can be turned on in order to work with a full head instead of half a head.*

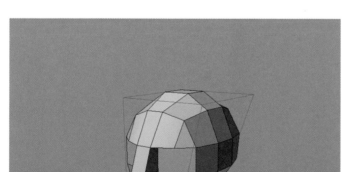

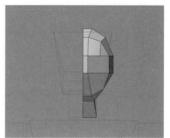

3. When adding edges for the eyes, create the eye socket area by extruding faces.

Also, tweak the nose and mouth using the **Polygon Split Tool** to add an additional level of detail.

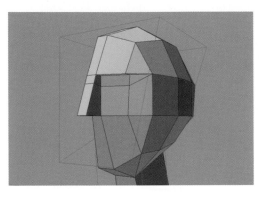
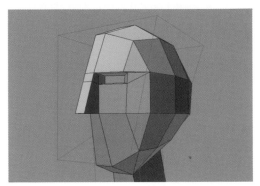
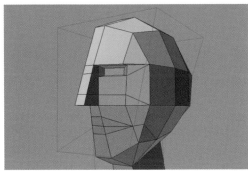
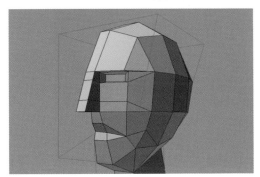

Adding edges to eyes

4. Adding details to the chin, eyes, mouth and nose

With each part of the face, make modifications by using **Extrude Face** and the **Split Polygons Tool**. At this stage some existing edges and vertices may need to be removed in order to move forward. This can be accomplished using **Edit Polygons** → **Delete Edge** and **Edit Polygons** → **Merge Vertices**.

When making adjustments to the face, proportions and shape are important while keeping in mind the overall look of the face.

Note: *Maya offers a wide variety of polygon creation and editing tools. Explore using different tools and techniques to achieve results. Some additional tools you may want to look at during this stage are:*

Edit Polygons → Duplicate Edge Loop *Edit Polygons → Split Edge Ring Tool*
Edit Polygons → Cut Faces Tool *Edit Polygons → Wedge Faces*
Edit Polygons → Poke Faces

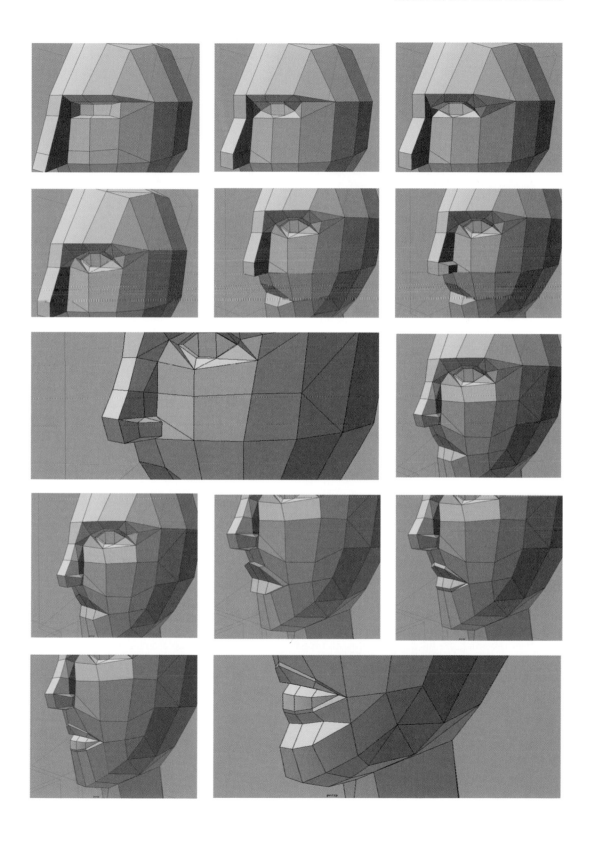

5. Having sculpted the eyes, mouth and nose, duplicate the model with a (–1) scale set to the appropriate axis in the **Edit → Duplicate Tools** options. Copy the other side of the head to examine the current overall result.

Although the diagrams shown below are only of the front and diagonal views, we should examine the head in greater detail by using the Perspective view to rotate and tumble the model in many different angles.

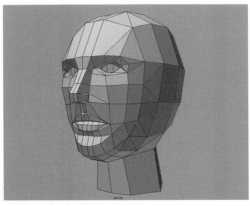 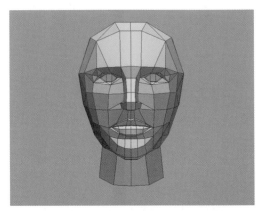

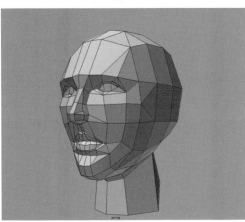 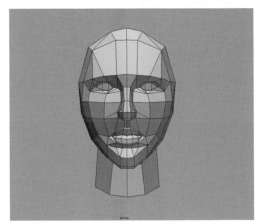

6. After reviewing the full head refinement, repeat the previous steps, delete one half as before and continue to improve the detail only on the one side of the head.

The diagram on the bottom of the following page allows you to better visualize the near complete eyes.

Be aware that when creating the eyelids, the upper and lower eyelids will overlap when the upper eyelid rotates down when the eye blinks.

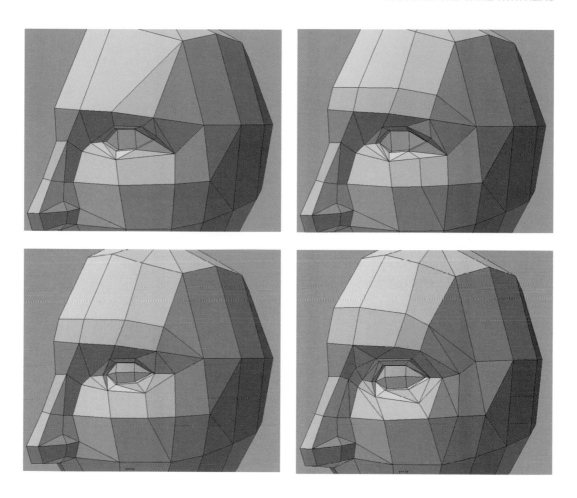

With this particular model, an interesting method is sued to model the eyeball and eyelid. In many computer graphics projects, the eyeballs of a character are modeled as separate pieces of geometry in the eye sockets. However, our model is a real-time game character, and the eyeballs do not move around. The eyeballs are modeled using a method that reduces the polygon count, while still allowing them to blink.

Eye detail

Using **Edit Polygons** → **Extract**, separate the faces that define the eyeball.

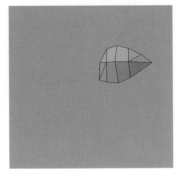

Using **Edit Polygons** → **Merge Vertices**, re-join the points of the lower eyelid. Then shift the upper eyeball edges to slightly beneath the eyelid.

This will now make blinking possible.

To better view the eye area, the polygons are reduced.

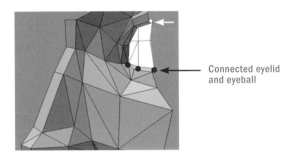

Connected eyelid and eyeball

7. When modeling the face it is important to be careful around the vital areas of the eyes, mouth and nose.

You should be cautious when modeling these areas, as they can drastically change the face's appearance, attractiveness and realism.

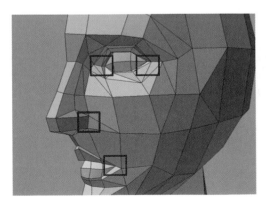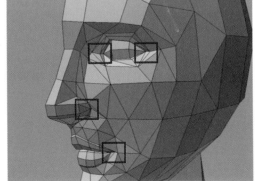

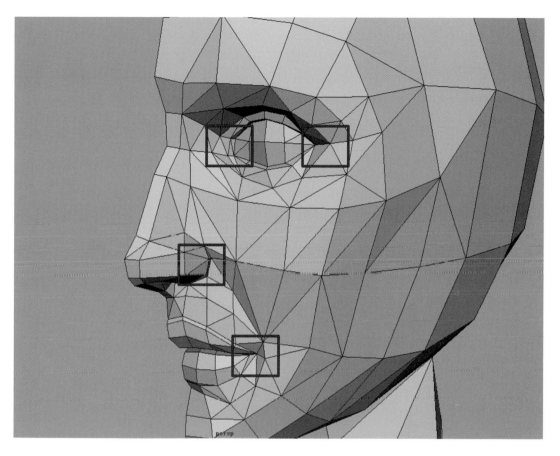

Because of the upper eyelid's wide range of up-down movement, such as when blinking, add a row of edges for interpolation when the eyelid shuts.

With this, the face model refinements are almost complete.

8. Using the same modeling method, we create the brow, ears, hair and hair topknot by adding more polygons using extrusions and splitting edges.

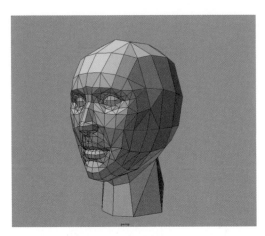
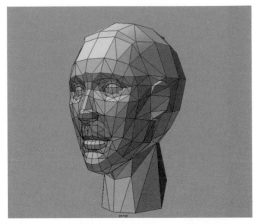

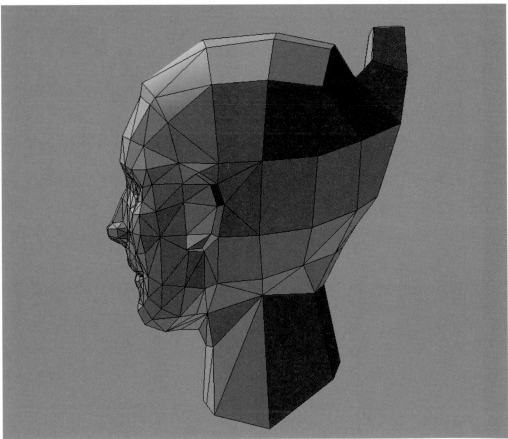

9. You will need to use the **Edit Polygons** → **Extrude Edge** to create flat polygons for the hair hanging from both sides of the head.

The hair is detailed with textures using an alpha channel, and consists of only flat polygons.

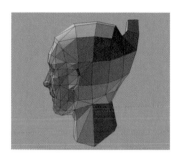

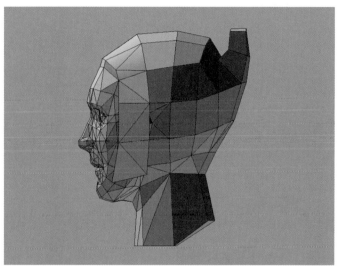

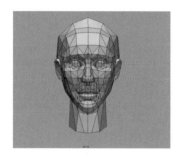

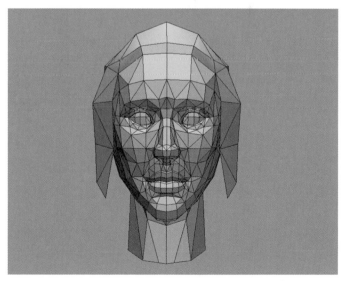

10. The head model is almost complete and it is time to begin modeling other body parts. It is possible to lose sight of the obvious when we focus for too long on one area. Therefore, after polishing the main body model, we will return to adjust the whole character model.

● Modeling the Body

Upper Body

1. Using the body primitive we modeled at the beginning as a template (see the diagram below), create a polygon cube that is proportionately divided into the different body parts. Similar to the work on the face, the arms, legs and neck are created using face extrusions from the upper body. Transforming vertices are then used to refine the shape. It may be necessary to split polygons to create faces for these extrusions.

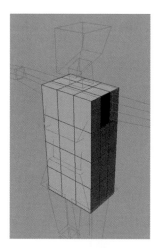

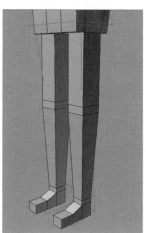

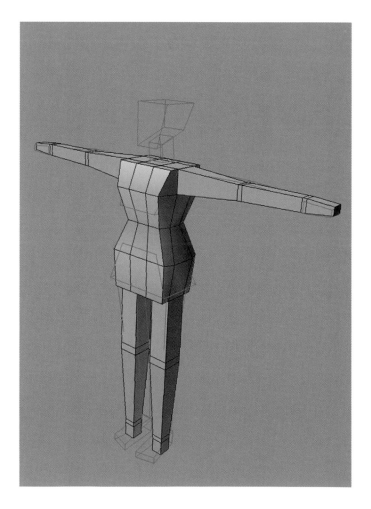

2. Continue to transform vertices to achieve the rough proportions of the waist and swelling of the chest.

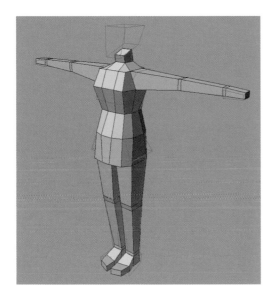 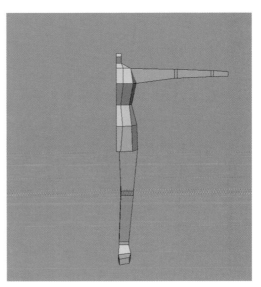

3. Once we have modeled the approximate body proportions, erase half the body and begin working on the other half, a step similar to the one used on the head model.

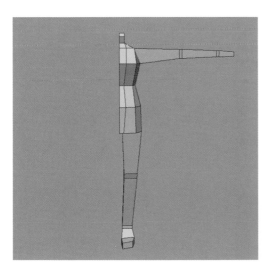

4. Using the **Split Polygon Tool**, add edges to the location of the collar.

 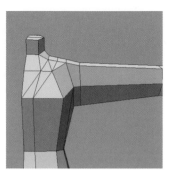 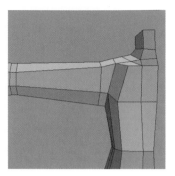

> **Note:** *A game often zooms in on a character. If we use only textures, a model looks blurred up close. Where possible, we use added polygon detail to compensate for any camera close-ups of the face and body.*

5. Add edges to create the arms' rolled-up sleeves. When doing so, transform the vertices at the sleeve to distinguish the arm from its sleeve.

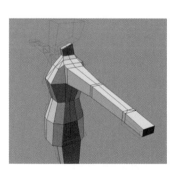

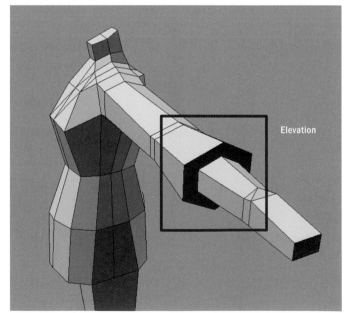

Elevation

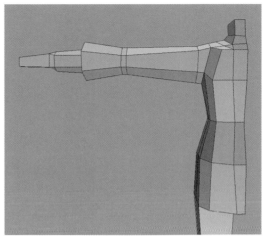

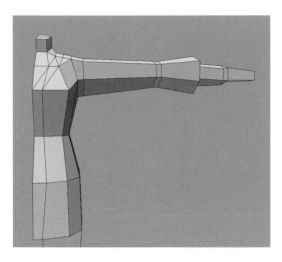

6. To create the sash, add edges to the hip. Now, create some slack in the clothing, while being aware of the chest above the sash.

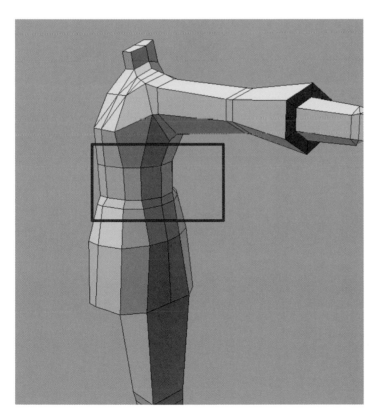

7. Improve the collar by splitting more edges to create detail and adding dimension to it by moving vertices.

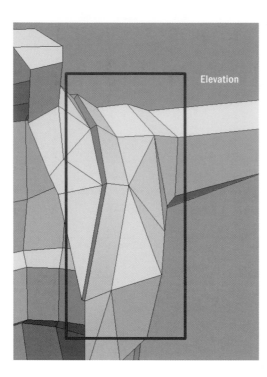

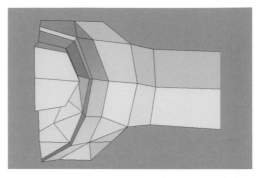

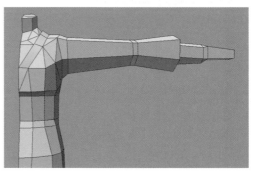

8. The shoulder is the body part with the most movement in the torso. To allow for this movement, add edges from the sides of the upper arm to the shoulder.

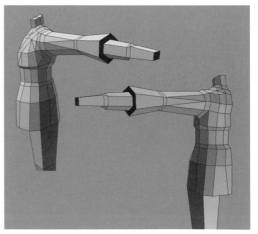

9. Now improve the arm. To correct its unnatural cylinder-like shape, continue to improve the arm by moving vertices.

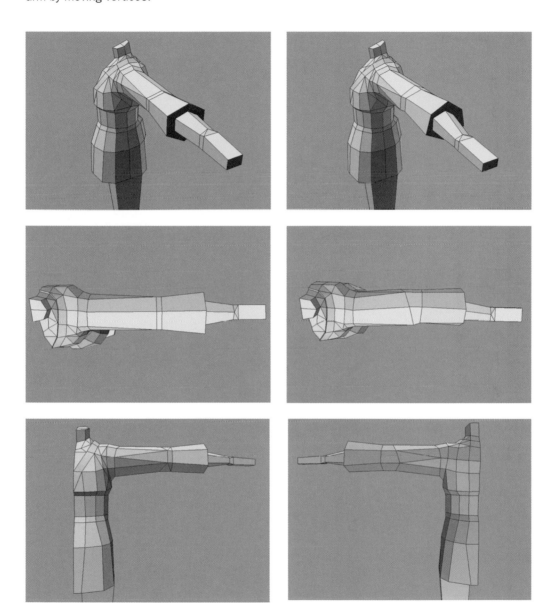

Before Fixes   *After Fixes*

10. Now improve the hand. Add edges to facilitate the faces for the fingers. After adding these edges, extrude faces to model the fingers.

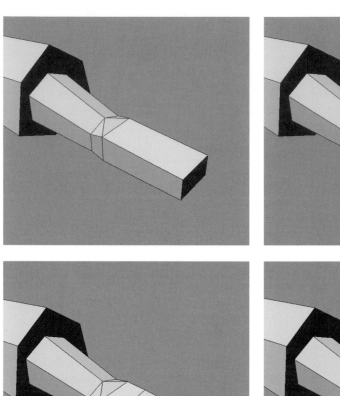
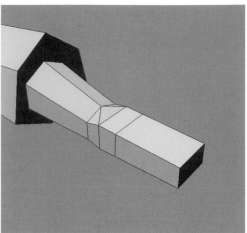
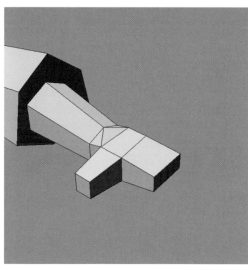
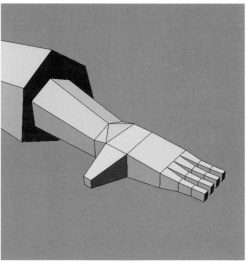

> **Alias** *Treat the Maya interface like it is a video game. A video game controller doesn't*
> **Tip:** *require the user to hunt for controls because it conditions you on how to use it.*
> *Maya does the same thing. The combination of the hotbox and marking menus*
> *allow a user to quickly maneuver between tools quickly without having to hunt*
> *for the right menu.*
>
> *Lee Fraser | Applications Engineer*

11. Add edges and transform vertices to adjust the hands' shape and size.

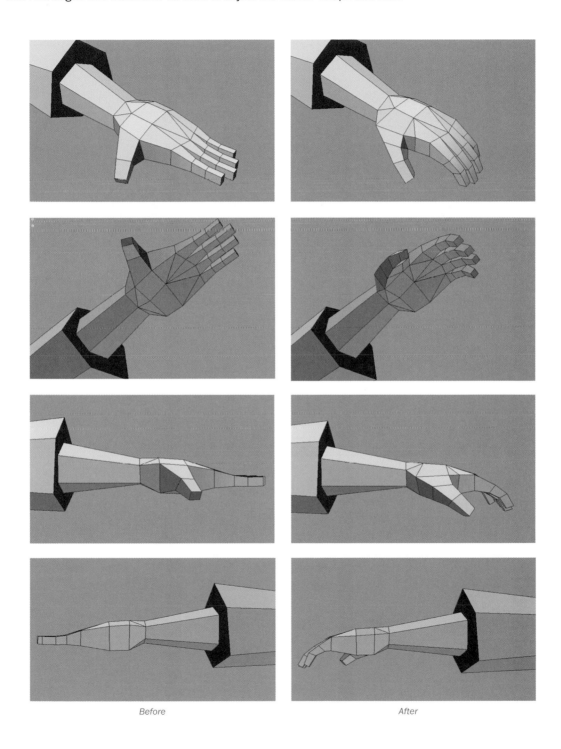

Before   *After*

12. Continue modeling the sleeve from the elbow to the back of the hand.

In an actual arm, there are two bones between the elbow and the wrist. To properly articulate the elbow and wrist motion, extra edges are added to the forearm part of the model. The arm will twist along the edges of the model to mimic a real life forearm muscle.

This model will not have bones in the individual fingers. Therefore, we give expression to the hand through the model itself. This character will be holding a weapon so there will be a pose between the hand holding the katana sword and the one not holding it.

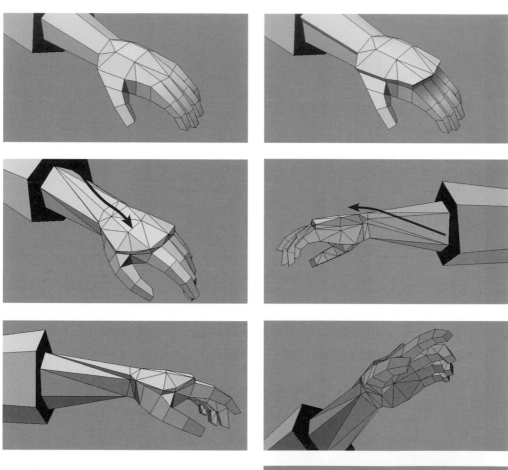

The upper body is almost complete. Next, we will begin modeling the lower body.

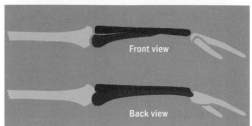

Lower Body

1. Using methods similar to modeling the arm, round the leg by adding edges.

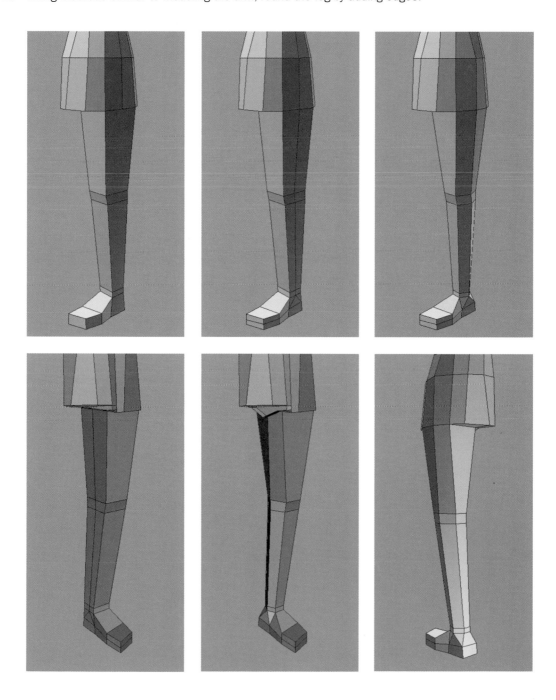

2. Edges are added to the calf and thigh, as well as to the hip area, as it also has a wide range of movement similar to the range found in the shoulder.

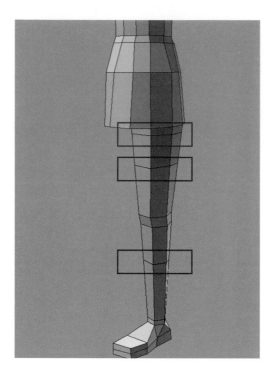

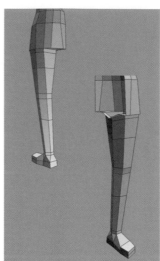

3. When setting up the final design of the model, the clothes of the upper and lower body will overlap each other. Using **Edit Polygons → Extract**, separate the upper and lower body at the waist and then again at the top of the leg.

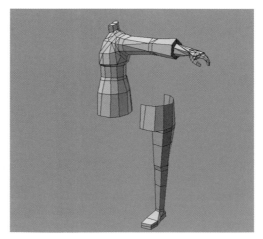

4. Shape the lower body from the buttocks to the thigh, incorporating it into the upper body.

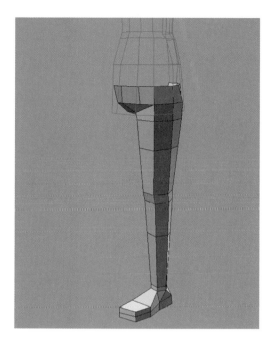
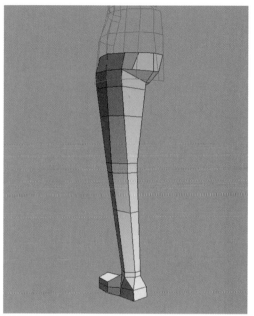

5. While shaping the upper and lower body parts, add more edges. Continue modeling while checking the positions of the calf, knee and thigh, ect.

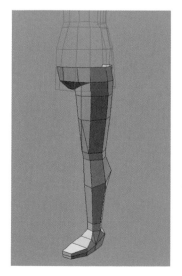
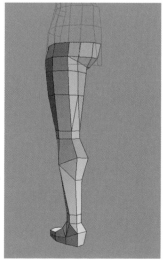
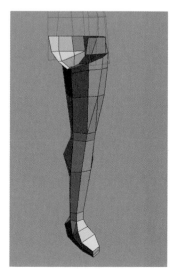

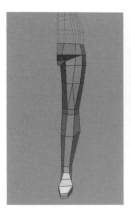
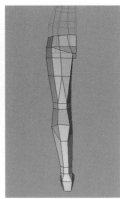
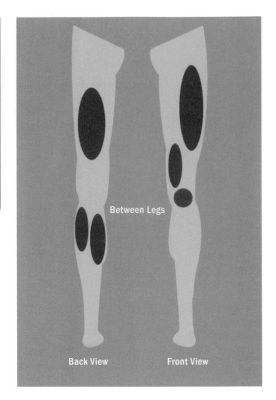

The calf and thigh muscles facing inwards are positioned lower than those facing outwards. Aware of these positions, we are allowed to model the muscles with increased realism and accuracy. The diagram approximately illustrates the position of the leg muscles. For more details, we recommend examining human anatomy reference materials.

6. Refine the model further. Often, the legs are shaped too straight and rod-like. Let the kneecap face slightly outwards, relative to the thigh and ankle. In doing so, this creates a more realistic leg-like arc. Be careful not to overcompensate in the kneecap. Overcompensating will bend the leg on the Y-axis and distort it.

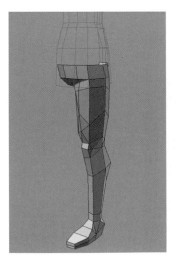
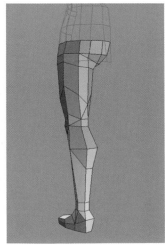
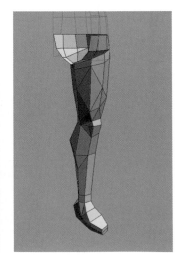

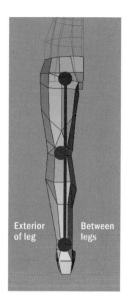

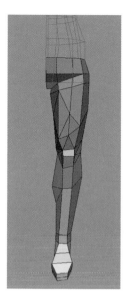
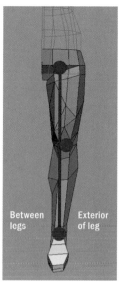
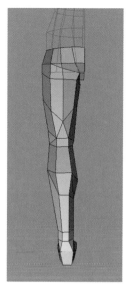

7. The character is wearing a pointy shoe on her foot. Split polygons and extrude faces as needed to model the shoe's pointed tip.

After tweaking the leg's overall thickness, we are almost finished modeling the initial character's shape. We will incorporate the face and upper body and then adjust the character's overall proportions.

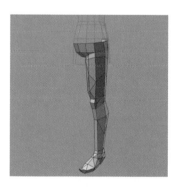
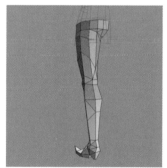
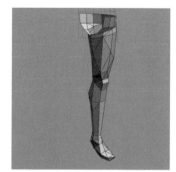

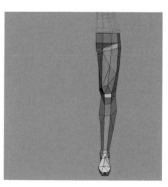
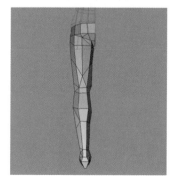
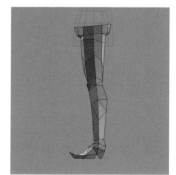

● **The Waist**

1. When beginning to add detail to the waist, ignore how parts of the lower body protrude with the torso.

A waist is greatly influenced by leg movement. Therefore, as we model, think about adding detail to the waist to allow for leg movement.

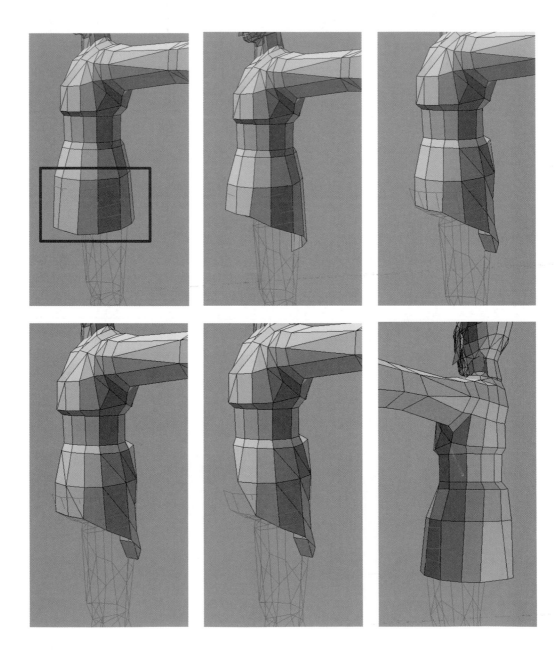

 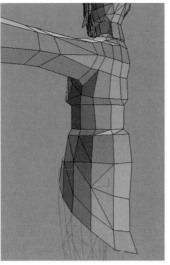  

> **Note:** *Some additional tools that can be used to make adjustments to the overall shape of the torso are within the Animation menu set:*
>
> *Deform → Lattice*
> *Deform → Non-linear → Bend*

2. By transforming vertices in the torso model, we will arch the back. In doing so, the buttocks become more pronounced.

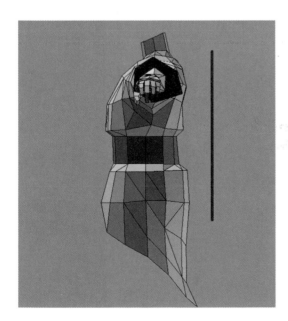 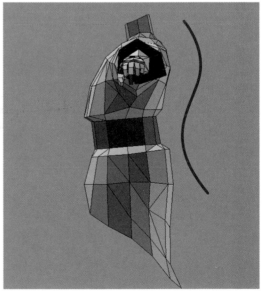

3. When a woman wears a kimono dress, the features of her chest can be difficult to distinguish so we will be exaggerating them by adjusting the vertices and edges. We will overstate many of the body parts to add character to the model, such as lengthening the legs and decreasing the head size. We will also add additional detail to the shoulder blade. Aware of the wrinkles caused by the shoulder blades, we split the edges on this part of the model. The overall mesh is nearly finished. We only need to balance the body proportions.

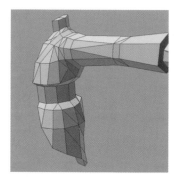
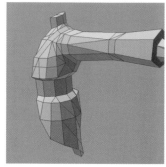
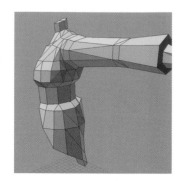

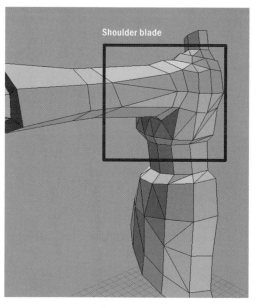

Shoulder blade

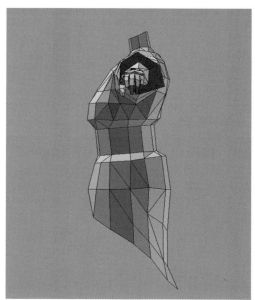

4. Sag is added to the back collar. We bring out the character's allure, showing the model casually wearing her kimono dress.

Final adjustments are made to the collar's shape by adding detail to the back of the collar, maintaining awareness of the neck muscles.

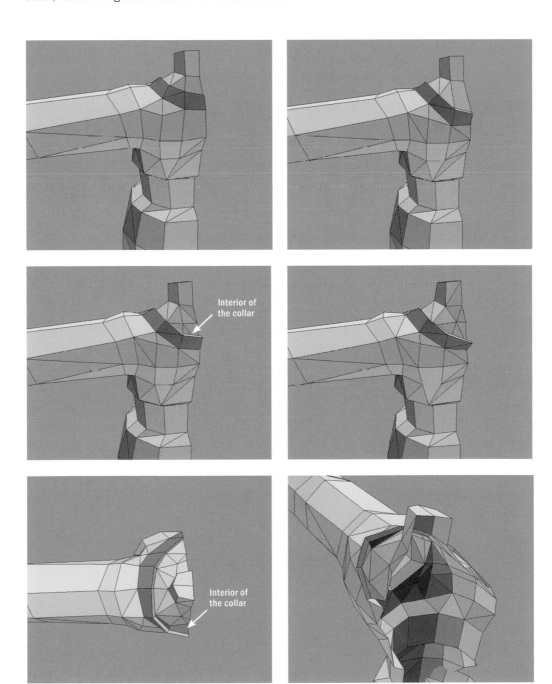

5. In regards to symmetry, the work is almost complete. From here, we will make adjustments (such as in the balance of the arm and the overall body proportions).

Areas fixed in our current model:

- Thickness was adjusted throughout the leg.

- Because the body is too constricted around the waist, the lower part of the sash was fixed. Also, the chest size was slightly adjusted, which is positioned correctly for the most part.

- The arm was adjusted because it was a bit too long.

- The head was adjusted, which was too large compared to the body.

- The protruding mesh around the buttocks was fixed.

Now, we have completed the foundations of our character model. We will continue fine-tuning the front flap of the kimono dress, as well as the model's sash knot, and create symmetry in the model. Afterwards, we will make final adjustments to the entire model.

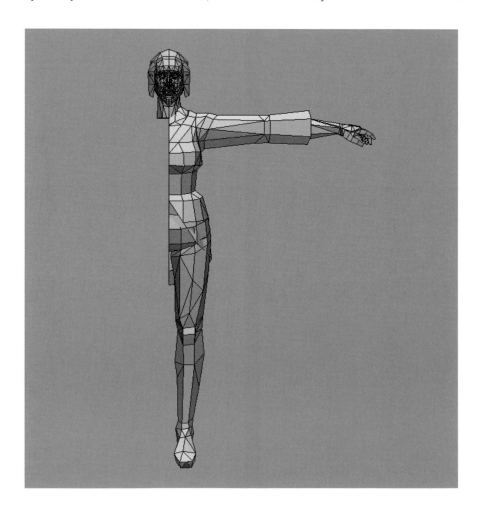

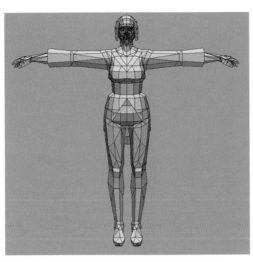
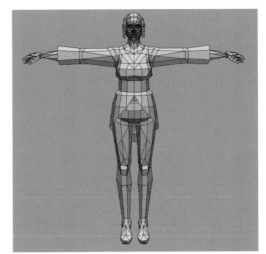

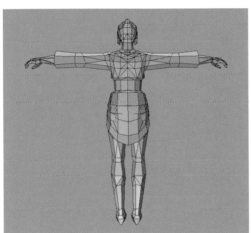
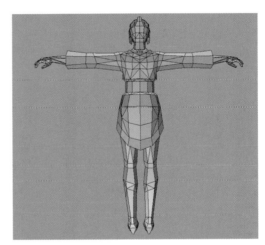

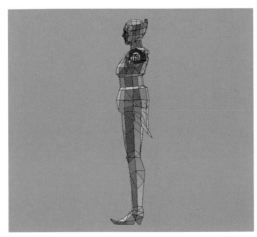

Before Fixes

After Fixes

6. Try to visualize a sumo wrestler's Shimekomi belt, or the excess length of a regular belt. The belt is wrapped forwards from the buttocks. The belt extends at the front and the belt extension sags down, creating the front flap.

In order to do that, start modifying the character model in the pelvic area, where the front flap will attach. This pelvic area will be mostly hidden by the kimono dress and front flap. We need to minimize the polygons used for modifications.

Though this not an immediate concern, the pelvic area may distort when animated. Just to be safe, add edges in this area.

When modeling any character model's pelvic area, we visualize the model wearing underwear. This allows us to model the legs to create better animations.

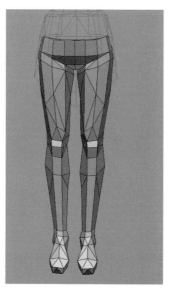

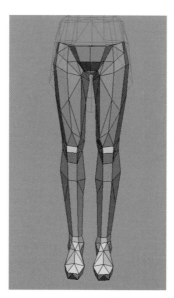

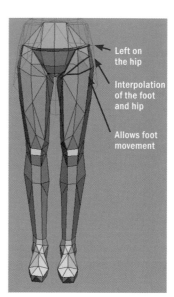

Left on the hip

Interpolation of the foot and hip

Allows foot movement

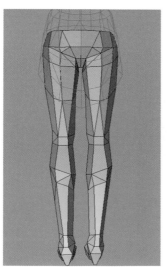

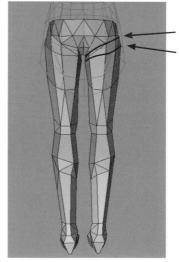

Left on the hip

Allows foot movement

7. Using **Create** → **Polygon Primitives** → **Polygon Plane**, create the polygon plane, which will be used to create the front flap. Rotate the plane by 45 degrees, and delete any unnecessary faces.

You should now be able to create the basic front flap.

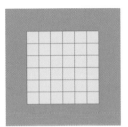 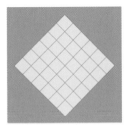  

8. Move the front flap to the character model's pelvic area. Using **Polygons** → **Combine**, attach the front flap's top right edge to the torso by matching it to the appropriate edge at the waist. Conceptually, the front flap flows from behind and inside the kimono dress.

Conscious that the character model's legs will eventually be animated, add detail to a few polygon faces in the front flap. Ultimately, the front flap will again be adjusted after the legs are animated.

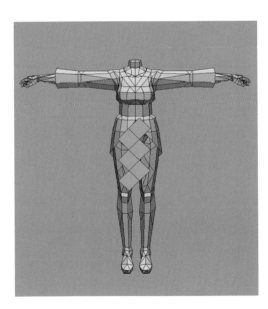 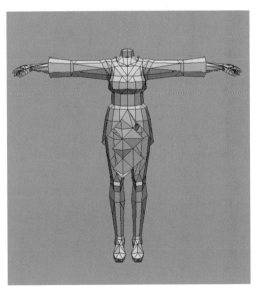

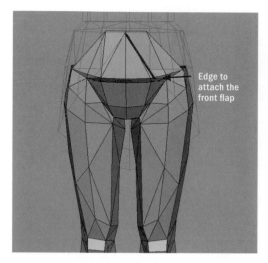

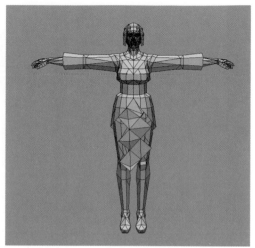

Edge to attach the front flap

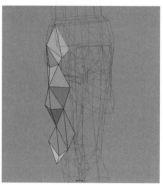

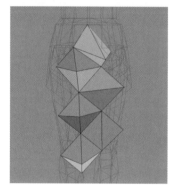

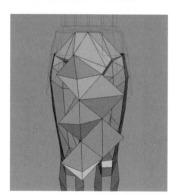

9. Before starting to create the sash's knot, adjust the buttocks and its polygon count.

To allow for leg animation, add edges to the buttocks. At the same time, we are conscious of the wrinkles when wearing a kimono dress. Thus, when animating the legs, greater realism is shown through the movement of the polygons.

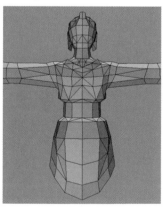

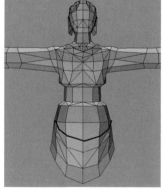

Before   *After added detail*

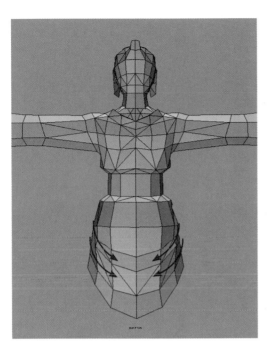
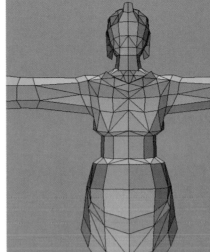

10. Create the sash's knot. Use **Create** › **Polygon Primitives** › **Cube** to create the initial knot shape, adding detail to add definition to the knot. Now make the lower part of the knot larger, giving the impression of sag from the knot's weight.

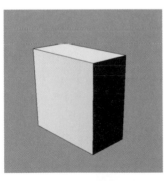
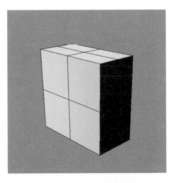
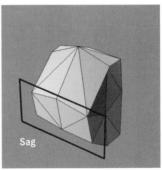

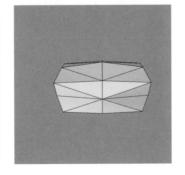

We move the finished sash's knot to the back of the character model's waist, matching it to the back's arch.

 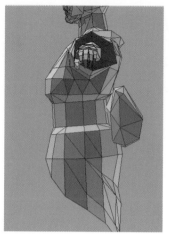 

11. Move the vertices to adjust where the sash's knot intersects with the body.

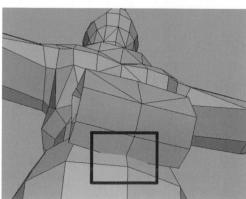 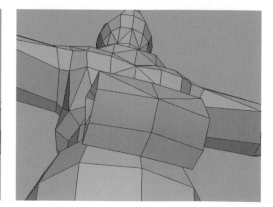

12. The torso and sash are not attached. To attach the sash's knot to the torso, create polygon planes to represent the knot end and the area where the knot begins wrapping around the torso.

The sash's knot appeared to be somewhat large, so it has been flattened. We attach new polygon planes to the sash's knot and the sash. We adjust the sash's knot to appear to flow from the sash itself. The area where we attach the sash's end will not be visible, and therefore does not need to be seamless. Attach the sash's end at the waist between the buttocks and sash's knot.

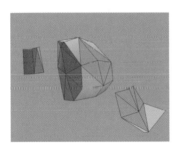
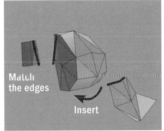
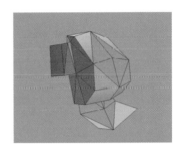

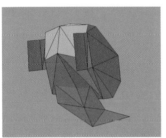
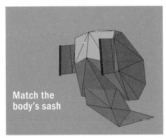

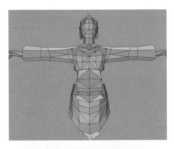

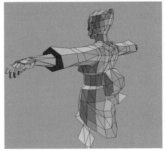

13. We add to the upper body asymmetry of the kimono dress so that it overlaps from left to right.

Shift vertices from the mid-body to the right to create an overlap on the kimono dress. Then, to make the fold of the kimono dress more visible, insert edges to add a ridge.

To create thickness in the collar, add edges and move the new vertices to create a ridge.

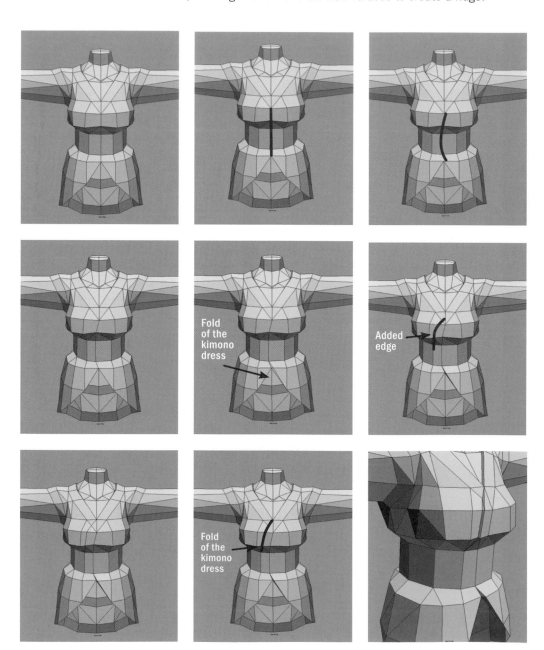

The 'valley' of the chest is not actually visible through the kimono dress. However, a valley is modelled to magnify its features. Move the vertices as needed to achieve the final result.

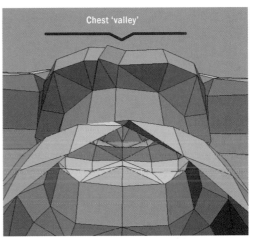

14. With the chest area almost complete, we will attach and work on the neck. From under the jaw, there are two neck muscles that extend and meet between the collarbones. Create those muscles by splitting polygons as needed.

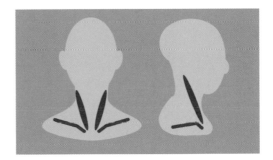

Adjust the features of the neck, such as its thickness, keeping it proportional to the other body parts, such as the upper body and the arms.

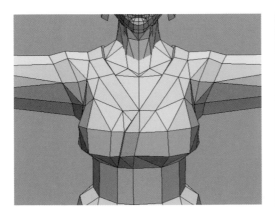

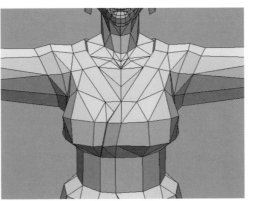

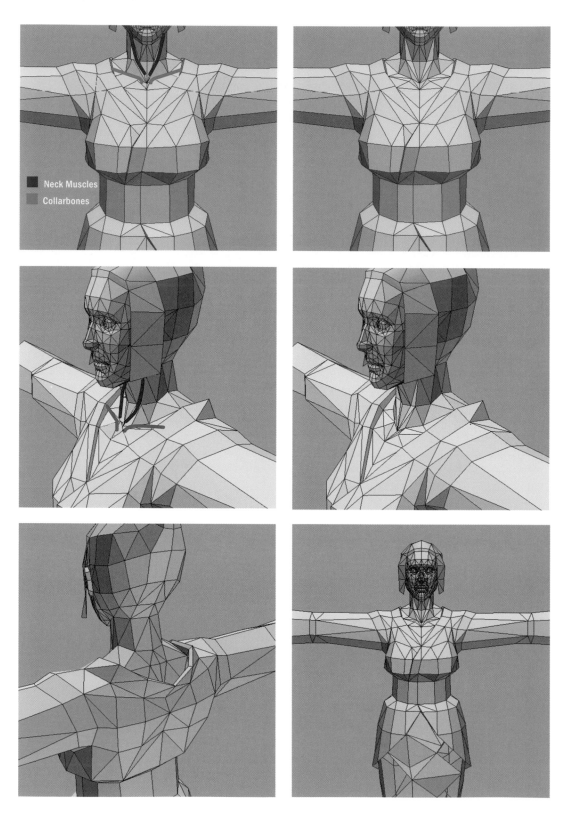

Neck Muscles

Collarbones

15. Next, we will be adjusting the lower body. The buttocks are hardly visible beneath the kimono dress and sash's knot. Therefore, delete the faces in this area. In doing so, this avoids the polygons from protruding through the kimono dress.

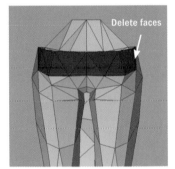

Delete faces

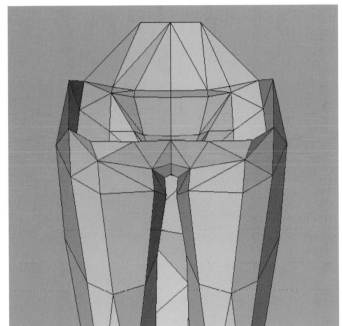

Front view

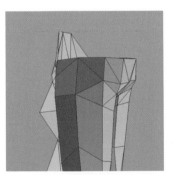

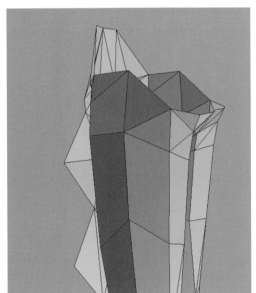

Side view

16. When polygons intersect with each other, such as with the buttocks and kimono dress, the number of points should be the same. In doing so, the polygons will behave the same when animated, which further prevents them from protruding out of one another.

For the present time, we have finished fixing around the hip by deleting a vertex in the lower buttocks.

● The Arms

1. Now the arms can be modified. Similar to the work on the head and body, only the left arm will be modified to ensure that both arms are identical after mirroring.

With the body parts identical on both sides, we still need to tweak the arms, face and legs in the same order - we erase one side, fix the other side and re-create the erased side with a symmetrical copy.

Early on, some body parts, such as the chest, may have been symmetrical on both sides. However, be careful to not accidentally erase your work, and not make these parts symmetrical again.

- To make the arm appear to be coming out of the sleeve, move the vertices at the end of the arm to the inside of the sleeve.

- To create a wrinkle effect during the animation, realign the edges that run along the upper arm to the elbow using **Split Polygon** and/or **Edit Polygon** → **Flip Triangle Edge**.

- Use **Edit Polygons** → **Merge Vertices** to reduce the polygons in the wrist area.

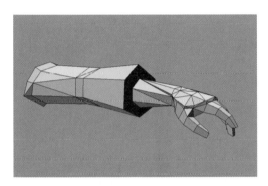

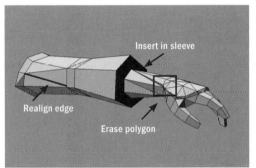

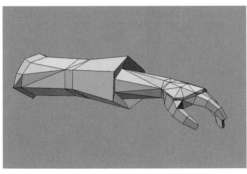

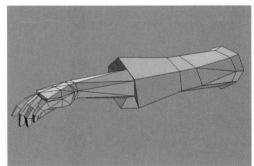

2. Further refinement to the appearance of the hand.

- Add a slight curl to all the fingers, excluding the thumb. Keep the middle fingers relatively straight and curve the other fingers towards it. The curve of the fingers should almost interlock.

- The thumb must not be too straight. As shown in the diagram below, twist the thumb into a loose S-shape that extends to the thumb's fingernail.

Paying careful attention to these subtle points, can give more expression to the hand, making the model more realistic.

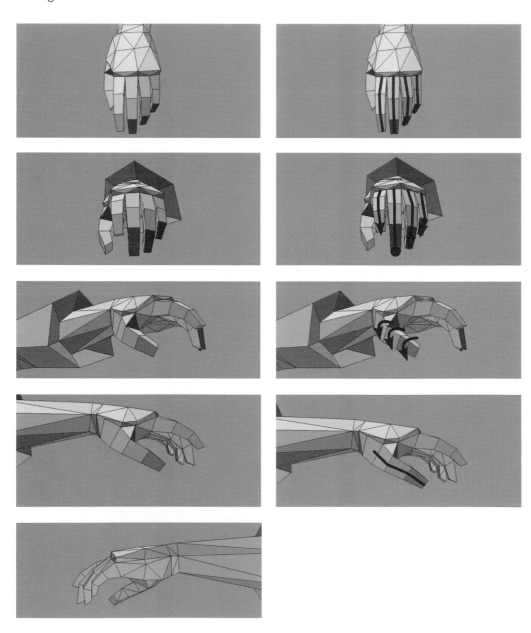

● Edge Normal Smoothing

At this point, use **Edit Polygons** → **Normals** → **Soften/Harden** to smooth the display of the model.

We have now finished modeling the character. The process of character modeling requires constant adjustments until the very end of a project.

The next steps are to begin character rigging, skinning and texturing, but we also continue to simultaneously adjust the mesh.

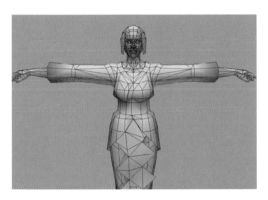
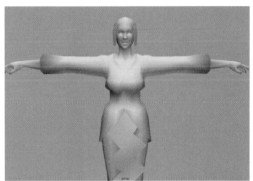

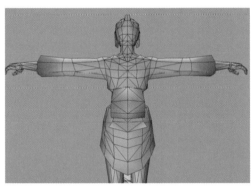
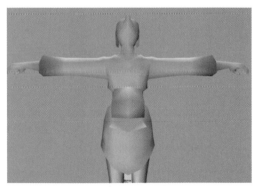

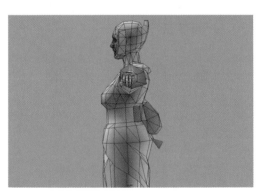
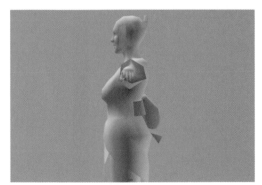

Section Two

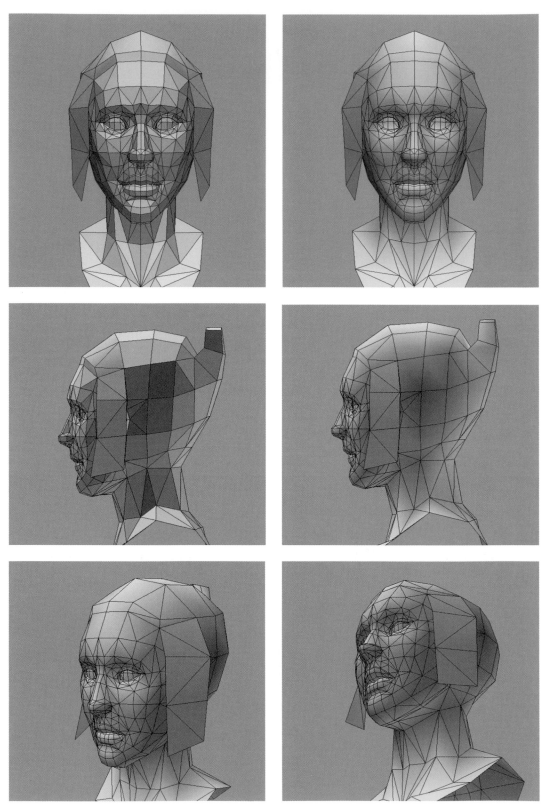

The finished head

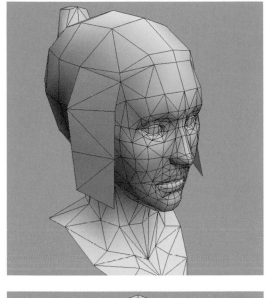
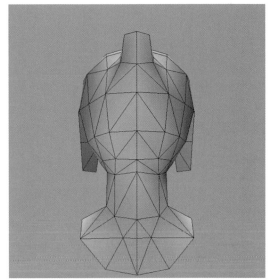

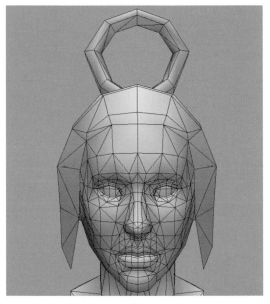
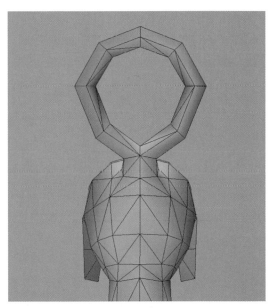

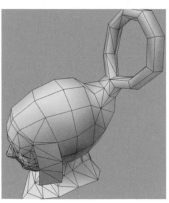
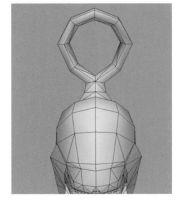
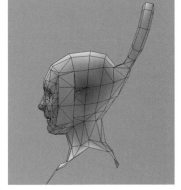

The finished head

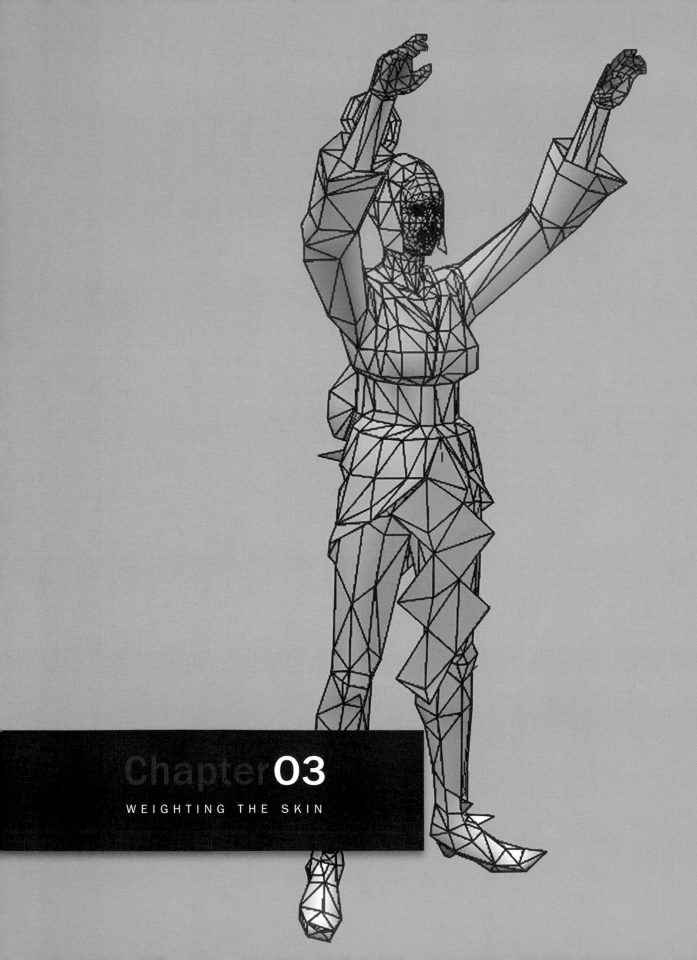

Chapter **03**

WEIGHTING THE SKIN

Introduction

Natural character movement is very important in video games. For that to happen, skin weighting is vital.

Weighting varies with each model, depending on the position of the points and the subtle differences of each polygon. Here, we explain how to approach weighting using our current character model. It is important to note, however, that this explanation may not work for all models.

We will animate our created model into various action positions, using repeated trial and error as the quickest way to achieve the best results.

● Basic Movement Check

The left diagram below shows the character model with all weighting at 100%, before the weighting adjustments. The right diagram shows it after the weighting adjustments.

Upon first glance, both character models appear to be well made. However, we will soon find increasing model animation problems without the weighting adjustments.

Let us now compare the key areas of the character models, before and after the weighting adjustments.

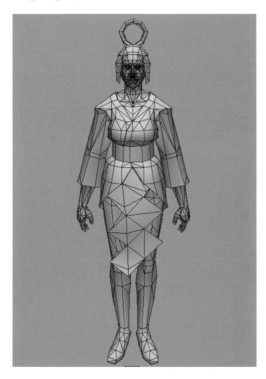

Before weighting adjustment

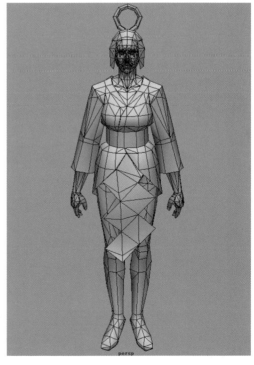

After weighting adjustment

Upper Body

In the upper body, the shoulders will require the most adjustment.

As stated several times during the modeling process, we can safely assume that the shoulders move the most in character animation. The shoulders have a variety of movements, such as rotating in all directions and twisting.

For these various movements, we proceed carefully with the shoulder weighting adjustments.

Our female character model wears a kimono dress. We redistribute the shoulder weighting a bit towards the arms. The kimono fabric will behave like a silhouette, with the shoulders not straining underneath the fabric.

The shoulder movement differs from underneath the clothes of say, a business suit. We have to compensate movement for the shoulder pads, leaving as much weighting in the shoulders as possible. As a result, the arms will not lower all the way, creating an impression that the clothes are inserted with shoulder pads.

In this way, the weighting changes our impression of a character's movements.

Therefore, while we may create an attractive character profile while modeling, we may also ruin or change it completely with the incorrect weight distribution.

Within Maya, several tools can be used to adjust skin weighting. After smooth skinning the character, use **Skin** → **Edit Smooth Skin** → **Paint Skin Weights Tool** or the **Component Editor**, which can be found under **Windows** → **General Editors** → **Component Editor**, to adjust the skin weighting.

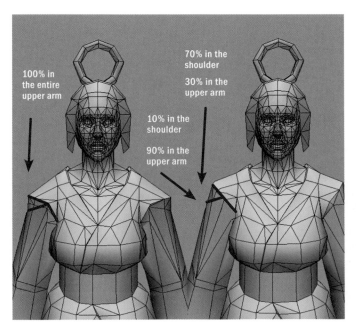

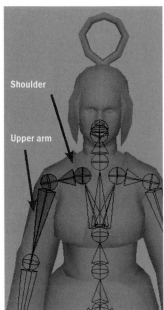

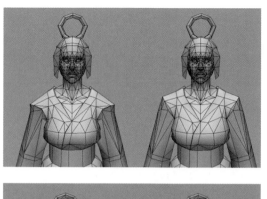
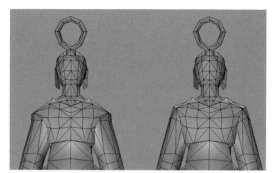
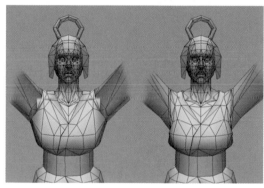
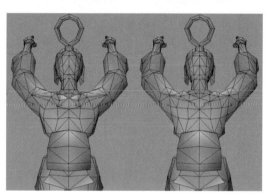

The chest and stomach vertices and faces also need to be adjusted. At this time, the model does not have the graceful movements of a human being.

The weighting to the chest and waist will also be redistributed.

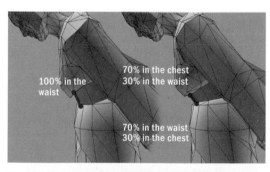

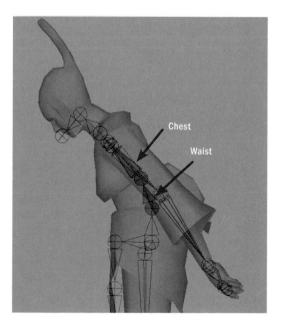

When relying only on the weighting at their center, the elbows may end up curling too much.

Therefore, make weighting adjustments, while being aware of the arms' profiles and joints.

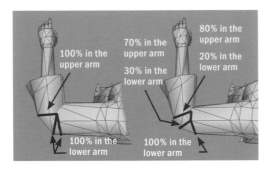

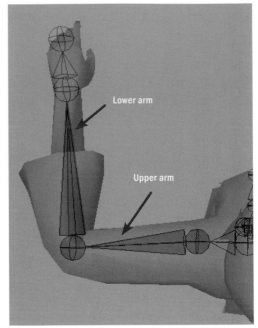

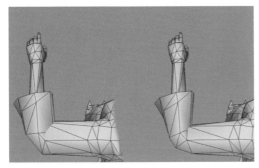

Lower Body

Not unlike the hip and buttocks areas, the front and back of the legs expand and contract the most, and have the most movement in the lower body.

These areas of the model are easiest to break down. Therefore, while ensuring the model's integrity, we will try a number of different leg poses while redistributing the weighting.

The lower body of a standing character model does not greatly differ from the default T-pose, which does not allow us to gauge where it is likely to break down. Therefore animate various everyday leg movements, such as stretching, walking and sitting in a chair. This allows us to see the problems we would not otherwise have seen, and to understand where we need to make our modifications.

When a movement is unique to a certain character, we will need to test it on the model.

Carefully redistribute the weighting for the hip joints and buttocks to the legs and root joint (or the top of the skeleton hierarchy).

We will also need to redistribute the weighting so the buttocks stick out when the character model bends over, and avoids the hip joints from intersecting.

Similar to the elbows, carefully redistribute the weighting at the center of the knees.

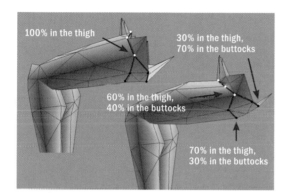

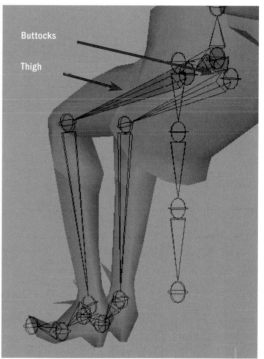

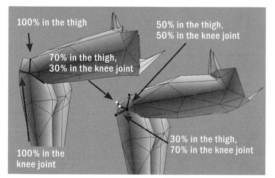

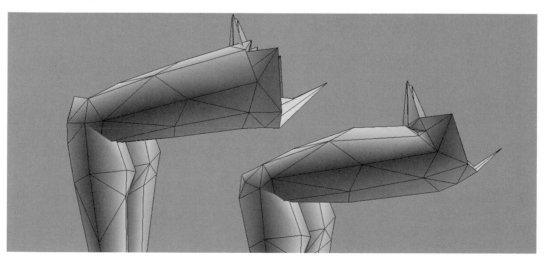

Two

The front flap has its own joint hierarchy. Modify and redistribute the weighting for the points in the joint influenced by any leg movements.

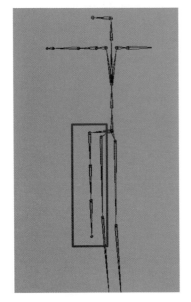

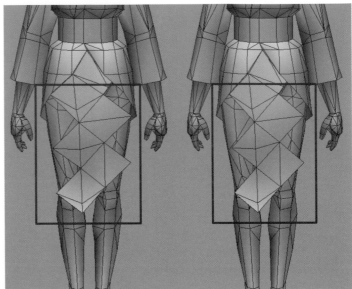

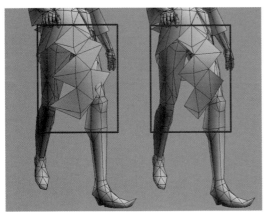

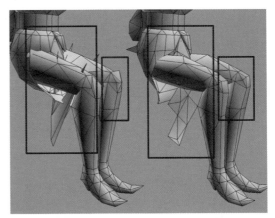

Alias Tip: *My biggest tip to a new user would be: "Learn MEL". At least learn how to pick out the pieces you want from the output in the script editor window. Then learn how to write a simple script which loops through multiple items in a selection list and does something useful. This will save you untold amounts of time. You should also know that holding* **Ctrl+Shift+Alt** *and selecting a menu item creates a button on the Shelf for you. Once you've learned that, you can take the time to learn how to create customized marking menus and hotkeys.*

Tim Fowler | Software Engineer

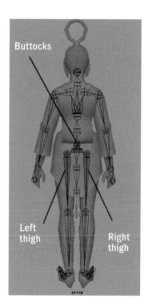

The buttocks and middle of the kimono dress are also very distorted.

The reason is that the four sets of bones in the legs - both hip joints, the root and the front flap joint - are influenced by them, resulting in uneven weight distributions.

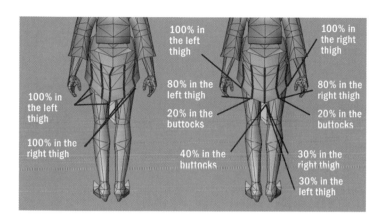

100% in the left thigh

100% in the right thigh

80% in the left thigh

80% in the right thigh

20% in the buttocks

20% in the buttocks

100% in the left thigh

100% in the right thigh

40% in the buttocks

30% in the right thigh

30% in the left thigh

Buttocks

Left thigh

Right thigh

We redistribute the weighting to the joint that causes the most influence.

In redistributing the weight, the center of the kimono may be problematic.

You will need to redistribute the weight of the kimono so that it is 'fan-like' along the legs and the root.

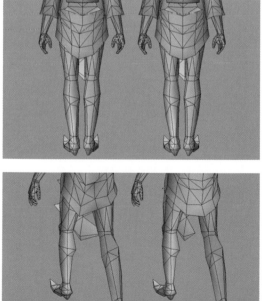

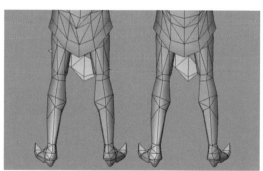

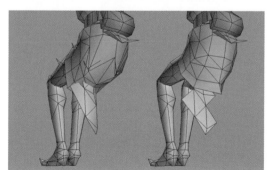

This concludes the explanation of weighting. In reality, weighting is an art form that is a difficult concept to properly master.

The preceding was only an example of weighting. To improve and fully understand weighting, we encourage you to create and adjust more characters beyond this book's explanation and examples. In the next chapter we will layout UVs and apply textures.

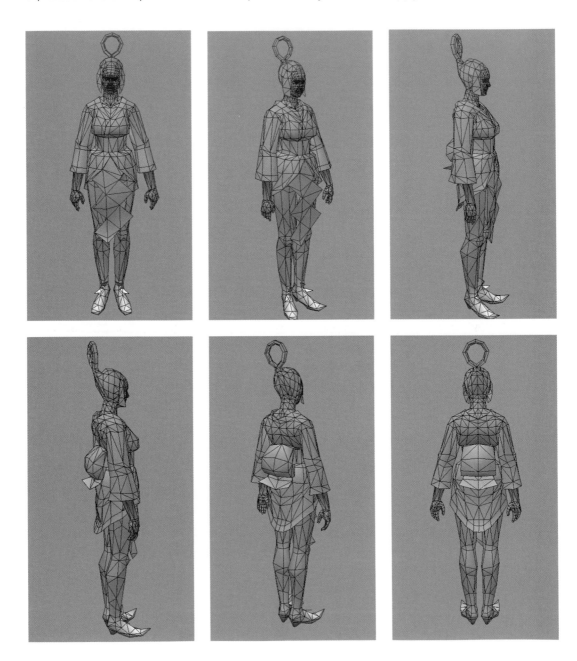

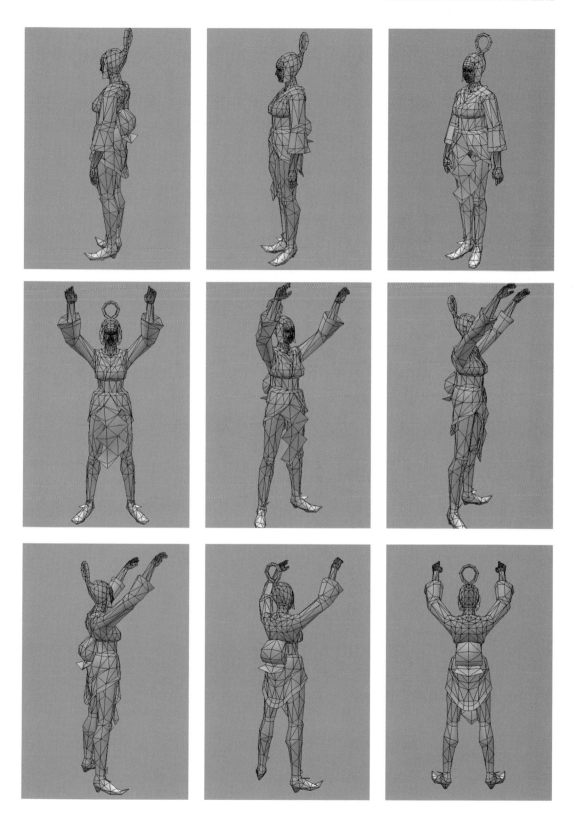

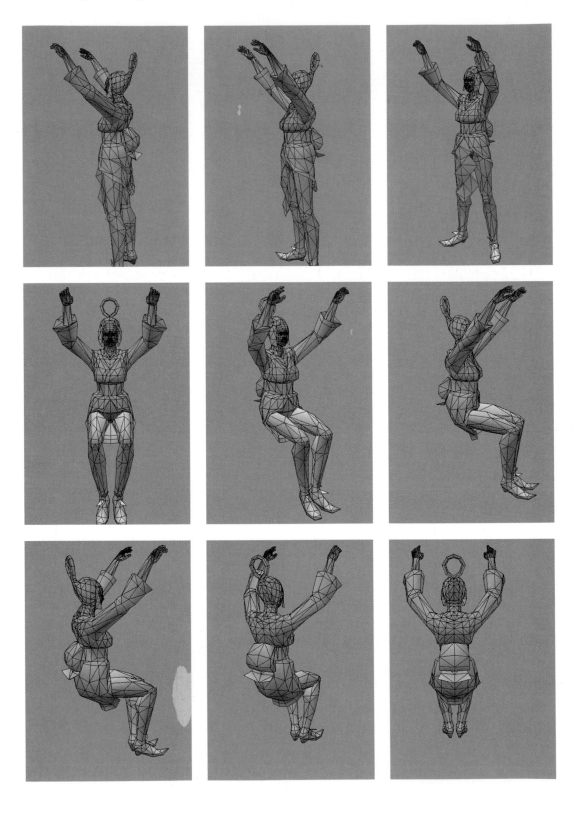

Chapter **04**

WORKING WITH UV TEXTURE

Introduction

In this chapter we will now layout UVs and begin creating the textures.

During game production, a texture should display the highest possible detail and with the lowest possible texture resolution.

From our experience, the standard texture size used for one character model is 256 x 512 pixels, but this varies depending on the game development.

When only two characters appear on screen, such as in the fighting game genre (*Tekken®*, *Mortal Kombat®*, *Street Fighter™*), we can concentrate on handling the two characters and change their texture sizes. Conversely, in a game where many characters appear on-screen, we may reduce the texture sizes per character.

We adapt these considerations according to the particular game development.

This time, the textures are created within the standard size of 256 x 512 pixels.

We proceed by learning texturing methods, such as how to share textures and use them more efficiently within a model.

● Details of the Textures Used and Their Wireframes

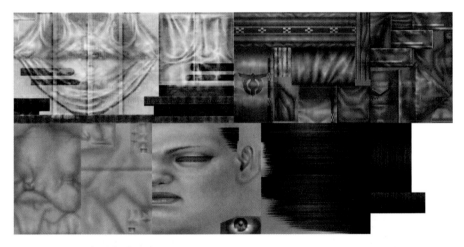

 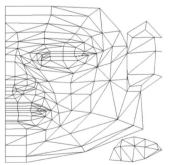 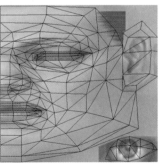

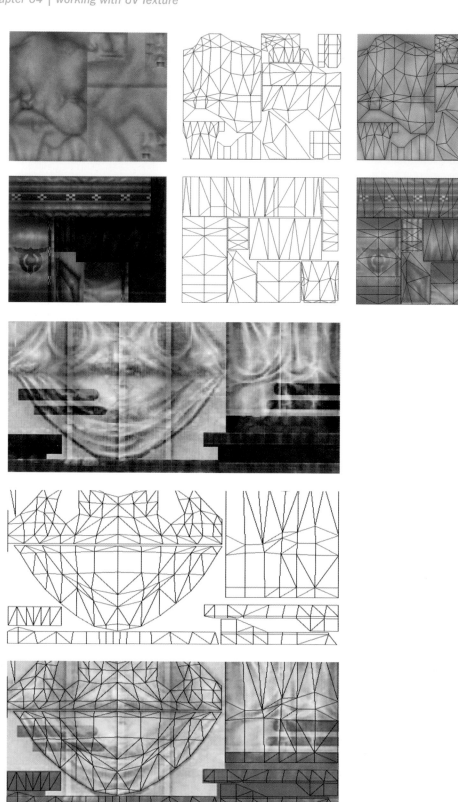

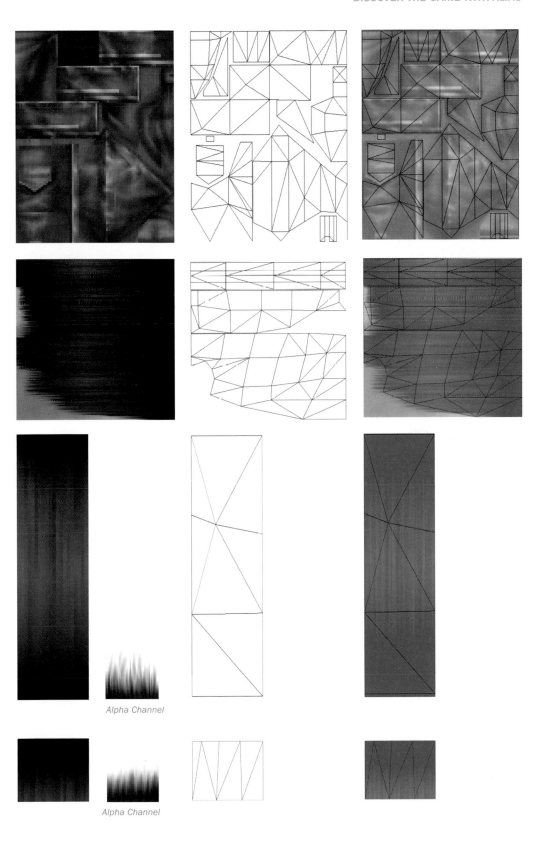

Alpha Channel

Alpha Channel

• UV Texture Coordinates

First, layout all the UVs and apply a shader with a checker texture.

This diagnostic shader is used to assess the texture sizes and to check for texture distortions.

Adjust the UVs attached to the model by using the various polygon tools and techniques in Maya. Afterwards, start individually drawing each texture.

As shown in the diagrams below, the checker detail for the head is a higher resolution than the rest of the body.

The need for higher resolution is due to the numerous times that the camera zooms-in on the head and its textures during the game. The details of the head textures have to be able to magnify under the camera.

If there are no fine details on the model's main body, the resolution of its textures can be lower, compared to the head textures.

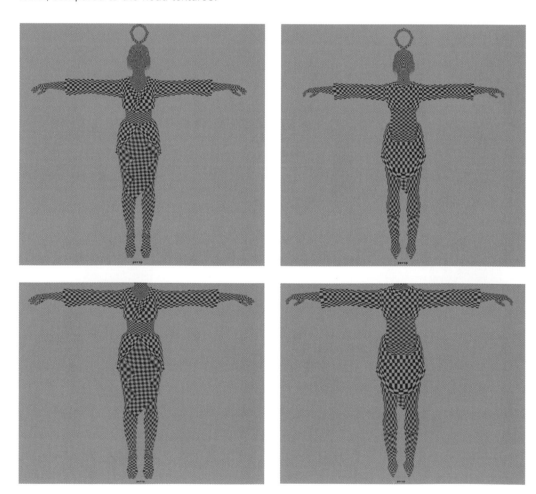

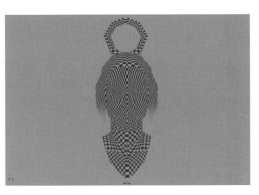 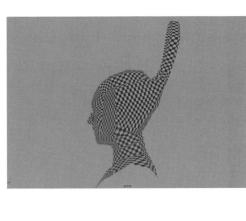

• Texturing Body Parts

Refer to the book's diagrams to see how we create the texture for each body part.

Head and Face

Even within the symmetrical face, she is textured with great detail.

Areas like the eyes, mouth and nose add to the facial features. Therefore, these areas need to be drawn with greater detail.

Conversely, since greater detail in the brows and cheeks adds nothing to the face, their texture space does not need to be as large.

Consequently, keep more UV space for the eyes, mouth and nose and allow for their texture resolutions to be able to draw in greater detail.

By efficiently redistributing the texture space conserved elsewhere, the eyeballs' texture sizes can increase.

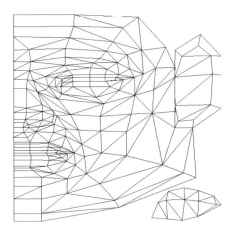
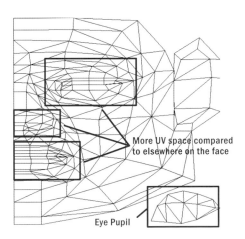

More UV space compared to elsewhere on the face

Eye Pupil

The hair was also created with symmetry. We removed the alpha from the hair that was hanging from the sides.

Section Two

*The parts of the used textures are highlighted.

Kimono Dress

Except for the sleeves, the kimono dress is to be asymmetrically draw.

The asymmetric texture patterns create the impression that the kimono dress is worn on top of a character's body.

Furthermore, the sleeves' symmetry is unnoticeable, being so far apart. However, when the two sides are closer together and more interconnected, like with the chest, texture asymmetry also prevents the wrinkles of the two sides from looking noticeably the same.

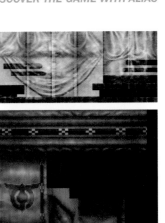

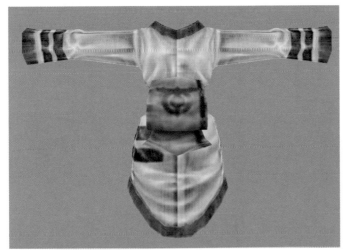

Where the polygon mesh is separate from the main model, such as the kimono collar, we are able to avoid texture distortions by placing the UVs to take advantage of the non-square pixels.

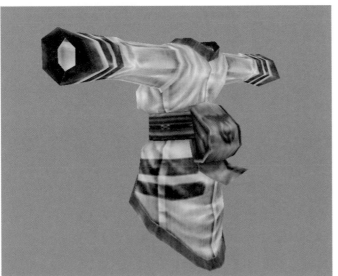

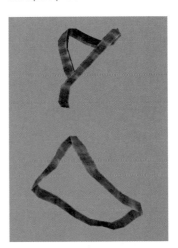

Arms

Similar to the sleeves of the kimono dress, the two wrist-guards are symmetrical.

Pay close attention to the fingers. The fingers have the same number of joints, and differ only in length. Therefore, the same texture is shared for all the fingers, excluding the thumbs.

Although the fingers use the same texture, once animated, they should not look uneasy together. The differing finger lengths also help.

The similarities of the finger textures can be disguised with the set-up of the wrist-guards. However, when the hand textures are created, we hide the texture similarities by matching the color of the fingers and knuckles.

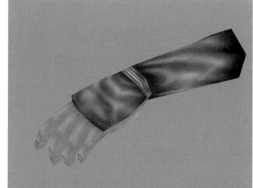

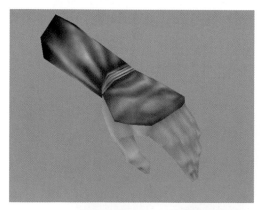

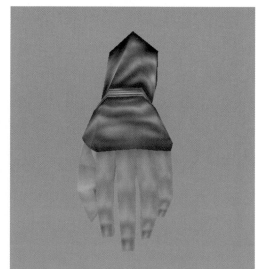

Lower Body

Except for the front flap, both sides of the lower body are symmetrical, and the textures are finished being applied.

Before and after applying the texture colors change the impressions conveyed by the model.

The model may look bloated and swollen with brighter colors of high color saturation. Conversely, the model may look constricted with darker colors of low color saturation.

When playing the actual game, the color contrast or saturation may be extremely high. The game development environment also changes the color characteristics.

Those color changes influence the actual impression of the character. Therefore, finish with character adjustments based on our impressions after modeling, weighting and animating.

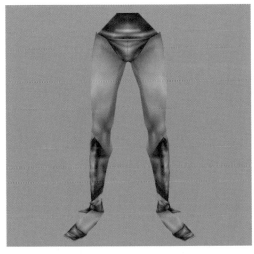

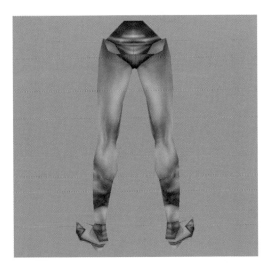

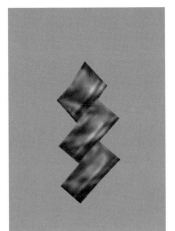

Final Adjustments: Addition of Polygons and Edges

Initially, we planned to only texture the tips at the top and bottom of the shin guards. However, with some flexibility left in the polygon count, and with our poor impression from only texturing the tips, a few polygon faces were added to the feet for the shoelaces.

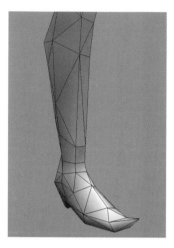
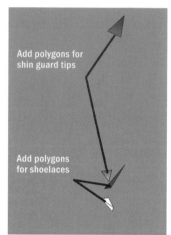

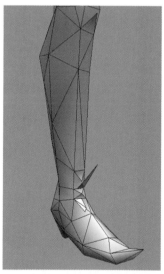
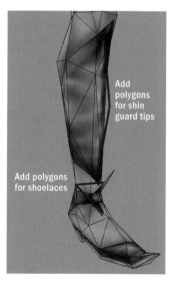

Alias Tip: *Take the time to understand the Maya architecture. If you understand the Maya architecture you will get all the power to free your creativity.*

Patrice Paradis | Application Engineer

More detail was added by adding polygon faces to the head by splitting the hair at the sides.

The textures for the hair at the sides were left unchanged.

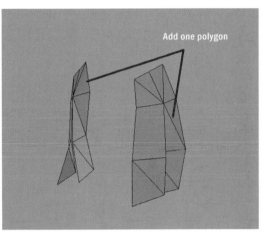

Edges were added to the middle of the kimono dress to prevent it from distorting when animated, and to convey a more graceful profile through it.

Mesh creation, weighting, UV layout and texturing are the fundamental steps in creating a character for a game. However, you will continue to make adjustments to the model until the very end of the project.

Only after working diligently to polish the model to our satisfaction do we make the it available for other people to use.

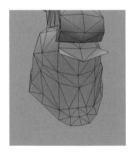
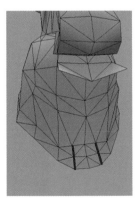

- **Finished Character Images**

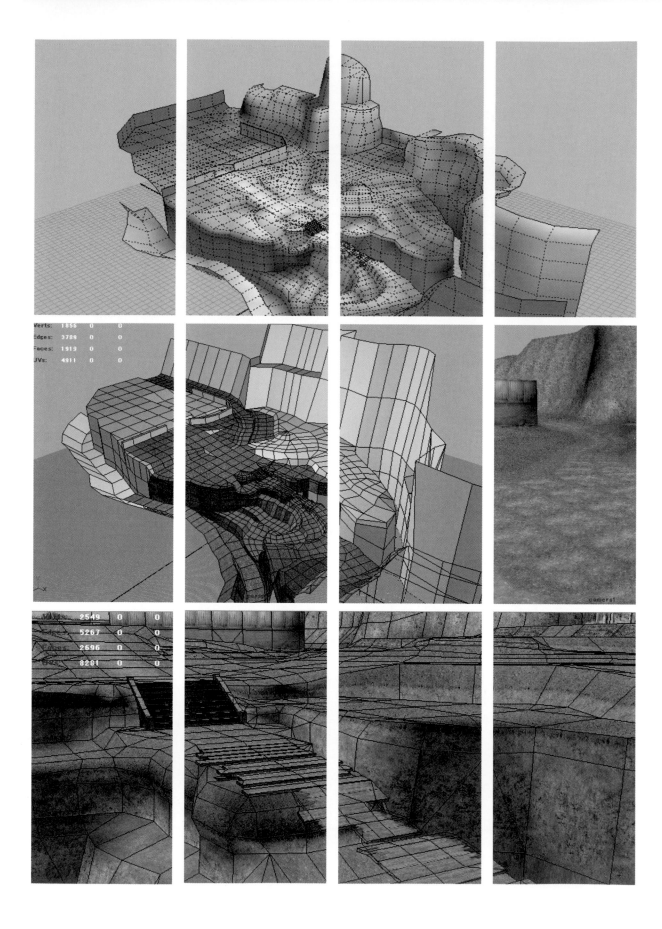

Chapter **05**

CREATING BACKGROUNDS

Introduction

When creating the ground, several smaller textures are combined into a more diverse, larger one.

A game production has restrictions for the polygon count, number of textures and size of these textures. We will first create the ground with as low as possible polygon count and number of textures, while still maintaining a natural look.

It is more efficient to improve the ground texture at the end of a game production with the unused polygons and texture space of other models.

Check the game specifications for the maximum polygon size, we'll also check the texture size to account for 1meter^2, whether it permits tileable textures and MIP maps, etc.

● New Terms in this Chapter

Normals – An indicator of which way a polygon is facing. It uses a vector vertical to the plane of the polygon.

Tessellation – A CG function that divides polygons into triangles to render a model on-screen.

Alpha Channel – The data that stores information of a texture's transparency level. The data is stored as an 8-bit grayscale or a 1-bit black-and-white texture.

Texture Sheet – Like a jigsaw puzzle, a sheet combining numerous smaller textures together. The sheet still needs to be within the game production's texture size restrictions.

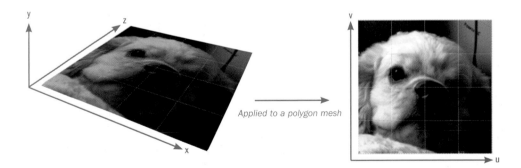

Applied to a polygon mesh

UV Mapping – A method used to map onto an object using a texture's UV coordinates (instead of the XYZ space coordinates). By adjusting the top-most vertices of a polygon mesh on the UV axis, we can easily apply a smaller texture to a texture sheet.

Tileable Texture – A texture that can be repeated when placed side by side with itself, analogous to conventional tiling inside a house.

Seamless Texture – A tileable texture drawn so all its borders are not visible when applied.

Vertex Alpha – A method that stores alpha information in the vertices of a polygon instead of a texture's alpha channel.

MIP Map – A CG function to use a high-resolution texture for an object close to the camera and a low-resolution texture for an object far away (from the camera causing it to appear smaller on-screen).

● Game Specifications

In a game production pipeline, initial tasks are to model and map the ground. However, we first need to understand its game specifications. The specifications detail how a game production will occur. They outline the many production limitations for setting up polygon geometry and textures for a background map. Though game specifications vary with every game production, its general concepts and principles are unchanged.

In this book, we will continue our explanation referring to our imaginary game production.

visual concept

> ***Note***: *Game specifications differ for each game production. The game specifications in this book are only one example.*

The Game Specifications

Village: map_001

CG Software: Maya 7.0

File Name: *map_001.mb*

Polygon Count: 1 map, maximum 20,000 poly
(measured as polygonal triangles)

Polygon Size: Maximum 5 x 5 meters when the camera
zooms in

Texture Layers: Approximately 20 256 x 256 pixel
sheets (when 256 color)

Texture Size: 8 x 8, 16 x 16, 32 x 32,128 x 128,
or 256 x 256 pixels

Texture Measurement: 1 square meter measures
64 X 64 pixels

Texture File Naming Convention

Color Channel Only:
m001_01_NAME.bmp
With 1-bit Alpha, m001_02_NAME.tga
With 8-bit Alpha, m001_03_NAME.tga

**Model File Naming Convention
(Distributed Object File Name):**
Normal No Restrictions

Instance (Distributed Object):
NAME_001
NAME_002

Background:
mo_NAME_a
mo_NAME_b
Sky sky_NAME
Cloud cl_NAME_a
cl_NAME_b

Alpha Priority Settings

Displayed from the top of a node (ordered furthest away from the camera)

Other Polygon Specifications: Maximum dual-sided and 4-sided polygons permitted

Other Texture Specifications: Maximum two tilings along either UV axis

Distributed Object: Use instance (at the original coordinates of (X, Y, Z = 0, 0, 0)

● Polygon Specifications: Converting and Counting Polygons, Direction of Edge Lines and Polygon Size

The game specifications measure the allowed polygon count of each map converted into polygonal triangles and the size of each polygon.

In the specifications of a typical game production, we ultimately have to convert the polygons into polygonal triangles or quads. The standard is to count polygonal triangles. Usually, the maximum is four vertices for each polygon. Therefore, we avoid using polygons with numerous sides (five or more vertices).

Converting and counting polygons

The basic flat polygon quad is counted as two polygons or two triangles.

4 polygons

9 polygons

12 polygons

When we include a multi-sided polygon

When we divide the polygons

When we divide the polygons into triangles for counting purposes

When a multi-sided polygon is incorporated into a model, the polygon may not be visible on-screen or may break apart. Even if the game specifications permit the use of quads, it is advisable to use triangles.

- ## Normals

A polygon also has normals. The direction of normals is moved to face a camera. A game's actual specifications may permit either one-sided (the direction of normals only) or dual-sided polygons. However, except under special circumstances, the direction of a polygon is moved to face a camera.

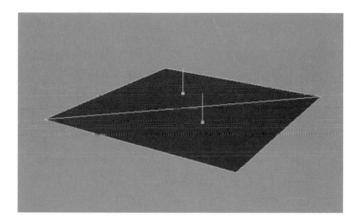

The direction of the edge lines travel perpendicularly from the center of the polygons

- ## Polygon size

Polygons have a maximum size. The game specifications outline the number of meters each polygon can represent for locations where the camera may zoom-in, in other words, the locations that a character may move up close to. The exact locations vary with the game production, and we should verify the game specifications. Without this information, the polygons may be too large in size and not display properly on-screen. A CG software function converts the on-screen game polygon into the optimal size of polygonal triangles. We call this software function *tessellation*. We have to work within the appropriate polygon size to use this software function. In other words, as we work, we check the game on-screen to make sure that an object is below a certain size when zoomed-in by the camera (except the landscape and anything else permanently distant in the game). Here, we work within a maximum polygon size of 4 – 5 meters.

● Texture Specifications: Colors, Data Size, Resolution and Size

The game specifications outline the allowed number of textures, texture resolution, etc. A game's overall texture memory is a certain number of megabytes. We calculate each texture's memory by dividing the game's estimated number of textures into the overall data size. Each texture size is usually 8 x 8, 16 x 16, 32 x 32, 64 x 64, 128 x 128, or 256 x 256 pixels - a multiple of 8.

64 × 64 pixels

128 × 128 pixels

256 × 256 pixels

64 × 128 pixels

128 × 256 pixels

Furthermore, the variants can be 8 x 16, 8 x 32, 16 x 32, 32 x 64 pixels, etc.

We also do not make textures full-color, but lower their color palette to 256 or 16-color.

When a texture does not have its own illumination, it needs an alpha channel texture, along with the common color channel layer (256 or 16-color). The alpha channel texture layer is in the 256-color spectrum from white to black, or just in black and white.

The former becomes 8-bit (2 to the power 8 = 256), and the latter 1-bit (2 to the power 1 = 2).

The former also does not have an alpha, and the latter is described as using both color and alpha.

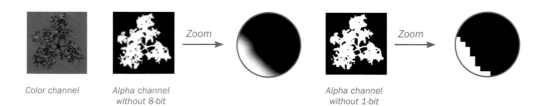

Color channel   *Alpha channel without 8-bit*   Zoom →   *Alpha channel without 1-bit*   Zoom →

When we enlarge the color palette, we also enlarge the game's overall texture memory. We have to lower each texture's color palette to the point that the impression conveyed by that texture is not diminished.

64 × 32 pixels

Please be aware that a 256-color texture has four times the memory of a 16-color texture.

128 × 64 pixels

> **Note:** *Texture sizes of 16 x 8, 32 x 16, 64 x 16, etc. are multiples of 8. However, these vertically long textures may take longer to load into a game and should not be used.*

Software reads information from left-to-right one pixel at a time, and is faster with fewer lines to read. Depending on the game specifications, we are permitted or restricted in the use of vertically (and occasionally horizontally) long textures. Therefore, it is important to verify these game specifications.

The texture resolutions are also determined in the game specifications. Here, we measure 1 square meter as equaling 64 x 64 pixels.

• Texturing: Individual Textures and Texture Sheets

When a game specification requires each individual texture to have only one piece of information (i.e. one texture design), proceed while carefully considering the texture's size, etc. With any game, each individual texture uses part of its memory (i.e. video RAM). Therefore, we sometimes combine multiple texture designs into one, to reduce the number of textures a game has to read.

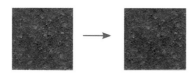

Even if we try to divide the 64 X 64 pixel texture into individual ones, it is still only one 64 X 64 pixel texture with one texture design.

When multiple texture designs are combined together like a jigsaw puzzle, they are called a texture sheet. A sheet still follows the texture sizes of the game specifications (square-shaped: 256 x 256, 512 x 512, etc.).

If we divide the 128 x 128 pixel sheet, we see that it is made up of four smaller 64 x 64 pixel textures.

Section Three

UV MAPPING METHOD

Combine textures into a texture sheet, and apply them through UV mapping onto a model.

1. Apply the texture to a polygon.

2. Add the UV information through projection mapping, etc.

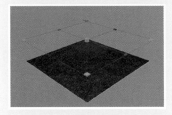 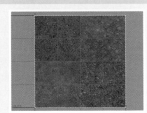

3. Move the UVs and UV map.

 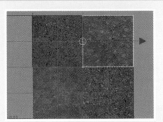

● **Mapping Tileable Textures - Tiling Seamless Textures**

Using a method of applying seamless textures is called tiling and it is used to create geometry with fewer polygons (low-poly) and textures.

Tiling is a texture mapping method where the number of times to copy and apply the same texture is defined.

Seamless means that the borders between textures are indistinguishable. Seamless textures are drawn to smoothly connect in all directions, when we repeatedly copy and apply them side-by-side.

On the left, the seamless texture is 128 x 128 pixels. On the right, that texture has been tiled three times in the 0 to 1 UV space.

When tiling, each texture sheet can have only one texture pattern.

Such as on the left, we cannot tile a new texture sheet from a pre-existing texture sheet. The resulting tiling pattern looks similar to the one on the right. We use individual textures (and not sheets) when tiling.

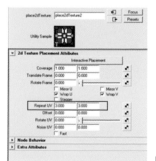

We also check the game specifications, as the number of tiles and the tile set-up differs with every game production.

Maya

We now define the number of times to tile the texture.

● Seamless Textures

If a seamless texture is drawn, the sequence-like pattern is noticeable when tiled. Therefore, a seamless texture with a simple design should be drawn.

Seamless texture

Tiled twice on the UV axis

Finished Image

Compared to (A), the pattern of the ground in (B) is noticeable and obvious. When we draw distinctive grass and rocks, they become visible patterns when we tile them as textures. For that reason, we draw seamless textures that are basic in design but do not detract from the realism of the ground.

A single texture (applied to one polygon)

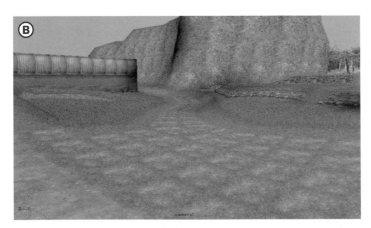

Seamless texture

Tiled twice on the UV axis

Finished Image

A single texture (applied to one polygon)

● Seamless Tileable Textures

Now, we will use a basic model to texture map and learn how to use seamless textures.

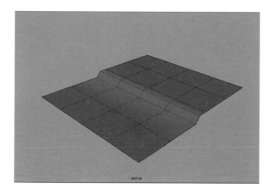

1. First, we model.

Create → Polygon Primitives → Plane → and to open the options and set **Subdivisions Width** to **4** and **Subdivisions Height** to **5**.

Adjust the vertices to shape the plane approximately like the image to the left.

| Sand | Grass | Details of the grass and sand |

2. Prepare the shaders and textures

In the Hypershade window create three new lambert shaders and assign the three provided textures to the shaders color channel.

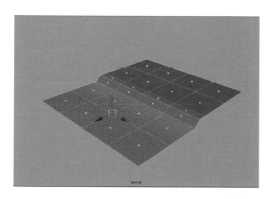

3. Apply the sand shader

Apply the sand shader to the appropriate faces.

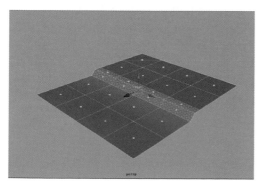

4. Apply the border shader

Apply the shader that borders between the grass and sand.

Apply the sand grass border shader to the appropriate faces.

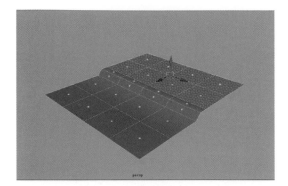

5. Apply the grass texture

Apply the grass shader to the appropriate faces.

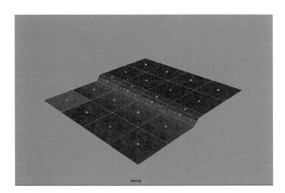

6. UV map

Select all the faces and use **Polygon UVs →**
Unitize UVs to map the UVs of each face to
the 0 to 1 UV space

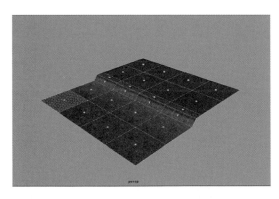

7. Tile twice on the UV axis

For each of the shaders created for this
lesson, a 2D texture placement node exists.
Within the attributes for this node, set the
Repeat UV to **2** and **2** for the sand shader.

Texture distribution   *Division of polygons*

8. Tile twice on the U-axis

Set the **Repeat UV** to **2** and **1** for the sand
grass border shader.

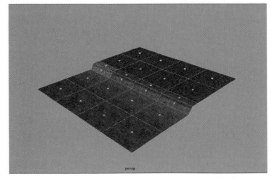

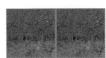

Texture distribution   *Division of polygons*

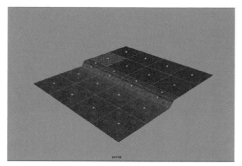

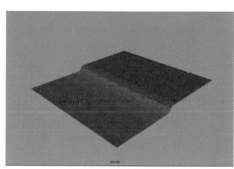

9. Tile twice on the UV axis

Set the **Repeat UV** to **2** and **2** for the grass shader.

Texture distribution   *Division of polygons*

10. Completed model with textures

In this way, we tile the ground's seamless textures along the UV axis, like the grass and sand textures. At the same time, we will tile along either the U or V axis, like the textures that border between the sand and grass. The sand and grass texture is a seamless texture between two other seamless textures. Several textures have been prepared and matched to create the ground.

If the game specifications do not limit the number of times a texture is tileable, we can tile seamless textures and prevent a texture from changing shape or stretching.

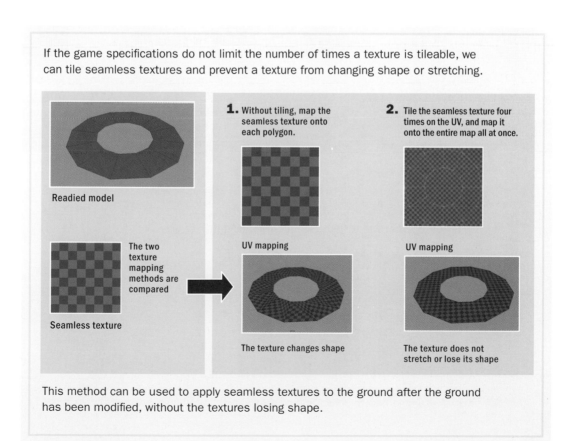

Readied model

Seamless texture

The two texture mapping methods are compared

1. Without tiling, map the seamless texture onto each polygon.

UV mapping

The texture changes shape

2. Tile the seamless texture four times on the UV, and map it onto the entire map all at once.

UV mapping

The texture does not stretch or lose its shape

This method can be used to apply seamless textures to the ground after the ground has been modified, without the textures losing shape.

Three

● **Characteristics of Seamless Textures**

Here, we use eleven 128 x 128 pixel textures and four 256 x 256 pixel textures.

Every seamless texture has unique characteristics:

1. The primary ground textures - tileable along the UV axis.

2. The textures connect to the main ground textures - tileable along the U-axis.

3. The ground texture connects the special locations - tileable along the V-axis.

4. The ground texture uses a vertex alpha - tileable along the UV axis.

5. The texture connects a primary ground texture to a special location - tileable along the V-axis.

6. The texture is not tileable along the UV axis, and does not connect to the primary ground textures, but connects along the V-axis to the texture of 5.

7. Individually or together, the textures are tileable along the UV axis.

Now, we will examine how to select and use the various seamless textures.

1. Primary ground texture: tileable along the UV axis

Seamless texture

Set to Tile Twice on the UV repeat attribute

Division of polygons

Finished image

Seamless texture

Set to Tile Twice on the UV repeat attribute

Division of polygons

Finished image

Seamless texture

Set to Tile Twice on the UV repeat attribute

Division of polygons

Finished image

Seamless texture

Set to Tile Twice on the UV repeat attribute

Division of polygons

Finished image

114

2. Textures that connect with the primary ground textures – tileable along the U-axis

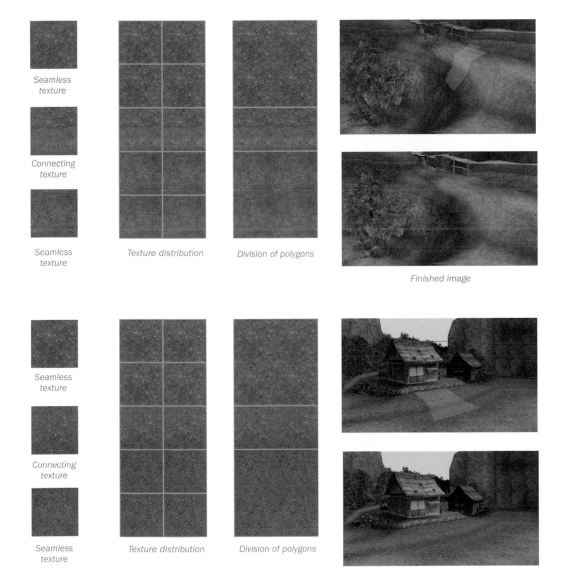

Seamless texture

Connecting texture

Seamless texture

Texture distribution

Division of polygons

Finished image

Seamless texture

Connecting texture

Seamless texture

Texture distribution

Division of polygons

Finished image

Seamless texture

Connecting texture

Seamless texture

Texture distribution

Division of polygons

Finished image

Seamless texture

Connecting texture

Seamless texture

Texture distribution

Division of polygons

Finished image

Seamless texture

Connecting texture

Seamless texture

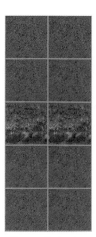

Texture distribution

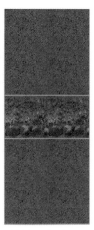

Division of polygons

Finished image

3. Ground texture that connects to special locations – tileable along the V-axis

Seamless texture grass

Seamless texture rock

Seamless texture gravel

Seamless texture path

Connecting texture

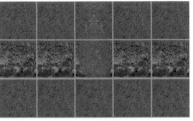

Texture distribution

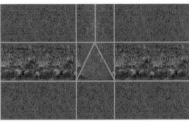

Division of polygons

Rotate the fourth seamless texture by 90 degrees and apply it.

Finished image

4. Ground texture with a vertex alpha – tileable along the UV axis

A vertex alpha does not place its information in a texture's alpha channel, but instead in a polygon's vertex. After the alpha value is set on the polygon's vertex, a gradual transparency effect becomes possible.

Maya

With the value '0' equalling complete transparency and the value '1' equalling complete solidity, we set our alpha values in the range between 0 to 1.

Use of the ground with illumination alpha

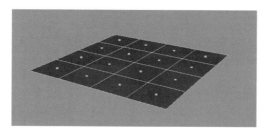

1. Create a 4 x 4 polygon plane.

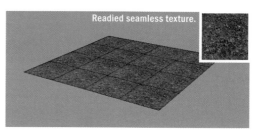

2. Create a shader with a seamless texture and apply it to the plane and layout UVs to tile it on the model.

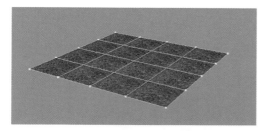

3. Select the vertices at the border of the plane and use **Edit Polygons** → **Colors** → **Apply Color Tool**, set the vertex alpha to 0.

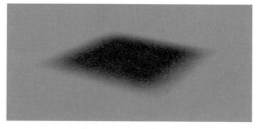

4. Make it non-transparent in the middle.

5. The ground area is barren.

6. Lay the previously created polygon plane with vertex alpha grid on the barren ground. Move the polygon plane slightly in the positive Y-axis.

7. It should look like the diagram to the left.

8. When prop models are laid out, such as trees, they benefit from looking integrated with the ground.

> **Note:** *The polygon plane will not display well if it intersects with the ground below it.*

9. The following is another example

How polygons are laid out

Finished image

Recently, some game creators have adopted a method of layering textures, called *multi-texturing*, to produce these types of results.

5. **Ground textures for special locations and tiles along the V-axis**

Seamless texture

Seamless texture

Tile on the V-axis

Texture distribution

Division of polygons

Finished image

6. **Ground textures for special locations that are not tileable**

Seamless texture tile on the V-axis

Seamless texture

Texture distribution

Division of polygons

Seamless texture no tiling

Finished image

7. Individually or together, the two textures tile along the UV axis

Seamless texture tile on the UV axis

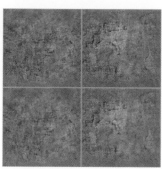

Texture distribution – division of polygons

Seamless texture tile on the UV axis

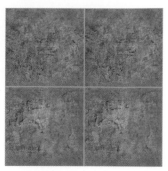

Texture distribution – division of polygons

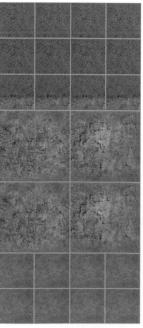

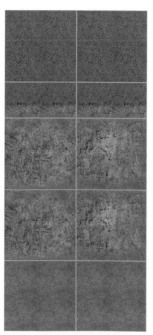

Finished Image

8. Practical application

Tile on the UV axis seamless texture

Tile on the UV axis seamless texture

Tile on the UV axis seamless texture

Tile on the UV axis seamless texture

Tile on the UV axis seamless texture

Texture distribution

Division of polygons

The ground was created by combining the seamless textures. Here, we used eleven 128 x 128 pixel textures and four 256 x 256 pixel textures.

Modeled and texture mapped, the ground is completed by finally adding lighting and illumination. Illumination is described in greater detail in later sections.

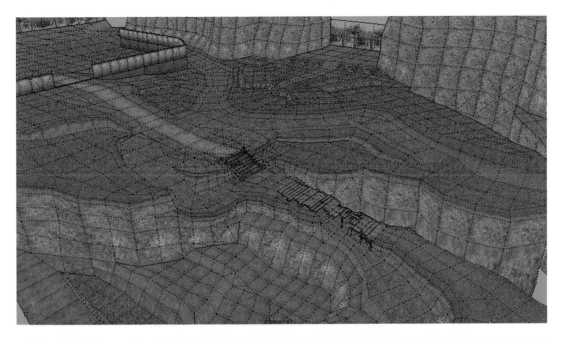

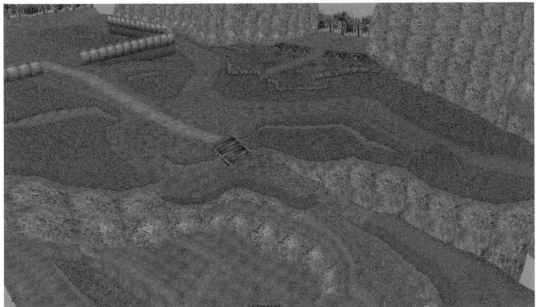

Without illumination

Illumination serves the role of a model's artificial shadows. It is very important, as it greatly affects a model's appearance.

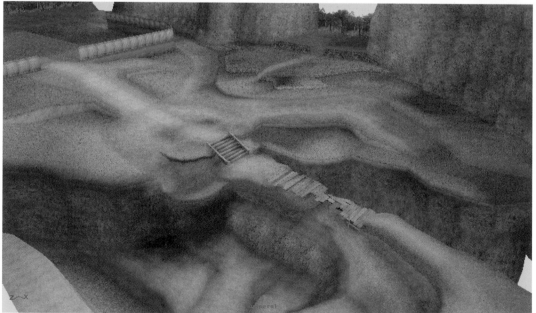

With lighting and illumination

• MIP Maps

The MIP mapping function automatically adjusts a texture to best suit its polygon's distance from the camera, and its polygon size on-screen. In other words, this function uses anti-aliasing to blur an object's texture when an object appears small to the camera. The texture's jagged edges grow more prominent with greater distance from the camera, but the distance makes the edges appear natural on-screen. This function has the added merit of speeding up the final rendering time.

The game specifications outline whether the MIP maps' textures are prepared by the creator or generated automatically by the game engine. The game specifications vary with each project and need to be verified.

Readied texture   *4 sizes of MIP maps*

Magnified

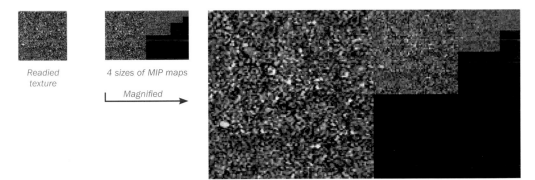

Notice the anti-aliasing and that the texture size is reduced by half each time

With MIP map   *Without MIP map*

Note: *Increasing the distance from the camera gradually blurs the details of the textures.*

Let us look at a texture where we can see the difference more clearly.

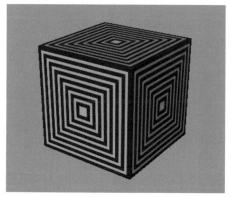

Readied texture

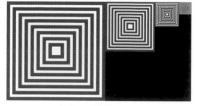

4 sizes of MIP maps

Noticeable jagged edges

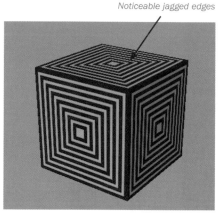

With MIP map

Without MIP map

A texture with comparatively prominent jagged edges, like a graveled surface texture, is high in color contrast. It may also be a texture drawn with many horizontal lines, such as a plank of wood.

When we are not allowed to MIP map in the games specifications, we compensate by drawing a texture with an already low color contrast.

Next, we will examine the actual production process for creating the ground.

● Production Process: Step 1

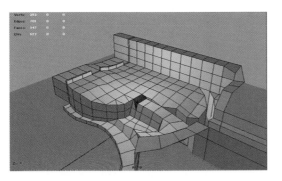

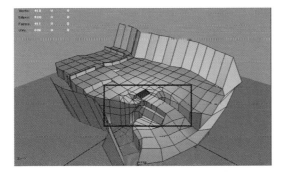

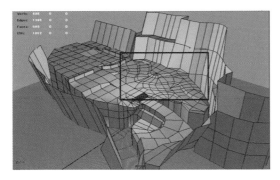

1. Model a basic level

Shape the basic terrain of the map using the various polygon modeling tools in Maya. Start with a primitive polygon plane and build up from there.

Gradually make improvements to the terrain.

First, add the central stairs.

Next, landscape the ground elevation.

Alias Set up your hot keys and your shelves to increase efficiency. It amazes my co-workers
Tip: when I show them something I do without having to scroll through the menus.

Albert Tam | API - MEL Specialist

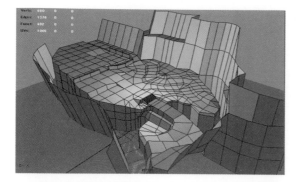

2. Assign shaders and textures

Decide on what ground texture to use and begin assigning shaders with these textures to the appropriate faces.

Categorize the location of each texture by color.

Following the game background specifications, follow the maximum polygon size of 4 meters.

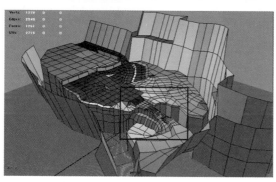

As a test, apply textures.

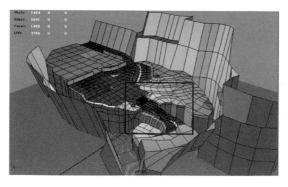

Refine the shape of the central bridge.

Texture map the central bridge and its surroundings.

3. Improvements

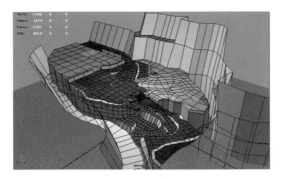

Continue texture mapping, while refining the shape.

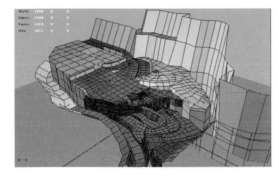

Further texture map the terrain.

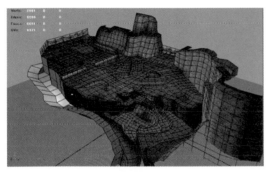

Make improvements to the rocks, using the same method as the bridge.

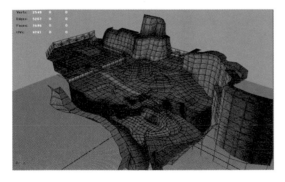

We have now finished applying all the textures.

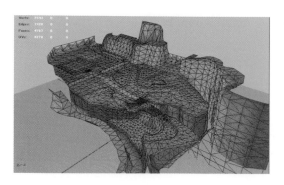

4. Check polygon count

After converting to polygonal triangles, check the polygon count.

There are 4,767 polygonal triangles.

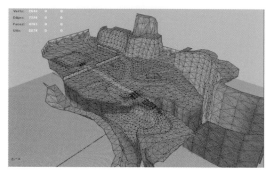

5. Adjust the color of the textures

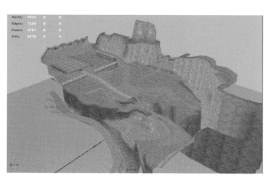

6. Complete the first stage

The work is complete for now.

All that is left is creating and positioning the other objects, while making modifications to the terrain.

● Production Process 2

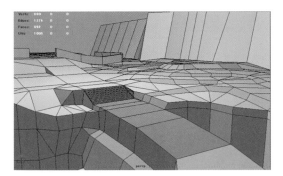

Focus in on the area of the basic bridge.

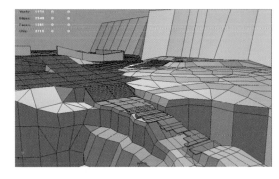

A more complex bridge will be modelled.

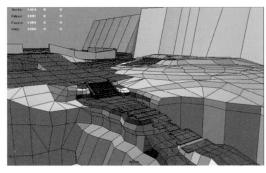

While making adjustments to the model, reapply texture maps as needed.

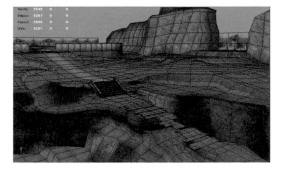

Here is the completed model with textures in wireframe in shaded mode.

● Production Process 3

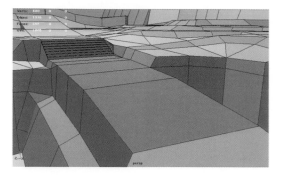

Frame the camera on the primitive model of the bridge.

Model the detailed bridge.

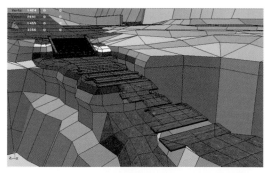

Apply the correct textures and UV map the bridge, while making adjustments to the model.

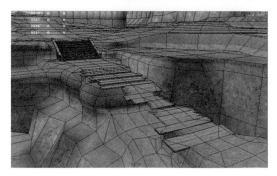

Here is the completed model with textures in wireframe in shaded mode.

• Production Process: Step 2

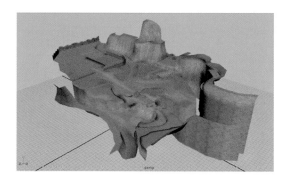

Finally, we will make adjustments to the project started in Production Process: Step 1.

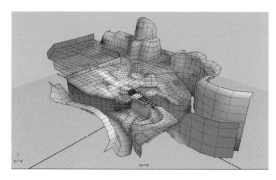

Add illumination through color per vertex, like the diagram to the left.

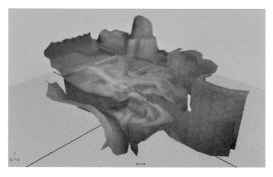

Here is a completed model with textures.

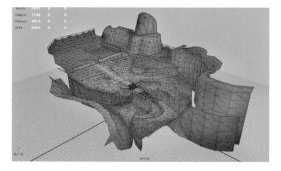

After converting to polygonal triangles, the total polygon count is 4,614 polygons.

Chapter **06**

CREATING A HOUSE

Introduction

First, we will calculate the polygon count total for one house by dividing the total number of houses. The total number of houses is outlined in the game specifications in chapter 05.

In situations such as modeling several houses, you usually need to first calculate the polygon count available for each house. You also need to calculate the overall polygon count and number of textures available for all the houses.

Without making these calculations, a background map's polygon count may exceed the game specifications, and require major revisions to reduce it.

An identical house model in the distance is unnoticeable. Therefore, we will improve the overall impression conveyed by the background by creating, copying and placing different house variations.

Similar to combining the ground textures, you can combine a certain number of textures to create many high-quality house variations.

UV mapping with a texture sheet will be used for the houses.

After unfolding an object's polygon mesh into a two-dimensional texture, UV mapping uses the texture's coordinates (U and Y), instead of the space coordinates (X, Y and Z). By moving the vertices of a polygon mesh along its UV coordinates, we can freely apply a texture sheet to it.

Polygon Count for One House

Here, assume the total polygon count for the level is 20,000.

We used approximately 5,000 polygons for the ground.

There are 15,000 polygons remaining. But, we need to create and place 12 houses. In other words, if we use 1,000 polygons for each house, for a total of 12,000 for polygons, we only have 3,000 left.

With this calculation, we are unable to place other objects (such as trees, grass, the main shrine and sky).

Therefore, re-calculate each house within 300 to 500 polygons. In other words, create all the houses targeting a total of 3,600 to 6,000 polygons.

Afterwards, with the remaining 10,000 polygons, we can create things found in nature, the main shrine, etc.

This is why it is good practice to calculate estimations before starting to model.

20,000	-	**5,000**	=	**15,000 polygons**
(total background polygon count)		*(ground polygon count)*		*(remaining polygon count)*

15,000 - (polygon count of one house X 12 houses) = polygons available for natural things, main shrine, etc.

For example, when one house is 300 to 500 polygons, we can calculate:

15,000 - (3,600 to 6,000) = 11,400 to 9,000 polygons

We have enough unused polygons to create the other objects.

20,000 POLYGONS TOTAL

Ground

Approximately 5,000 polygons

12 Houses

Approximately 3,600 to 6,000 polygons total (300 to 500 polygons / house)

Things in nature

Foliage, Rocks, Trees and Main Shrine (11,400 to 9,000 polygons)

In the end, the preceding numbers are only estimations. It is important to stay flexible in dealing with any game production.

● Scale Models

Here, assume that the game proportions are identical compared to general proportions in the real world.

Depending on the game, a character's height can vary from 75 centimeters to 125 centimeters.

We will create the game matching the height of a game level with that of a character.

Ideally throughout a game production, you should verify that a character and background look correct when placed together.

The proportions of the house match those of the character.

The character is too large relative to the house.

The character is too small relative to the house.

When creating the level, you normally place a character on it to check the proportions of their models and textures.

● Texture Resolution: Converting Real Measurements to Pixels

This book's texture specifications are 64 x 64 pixels for 1 meter^2.

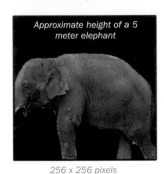

Approximate height of a 5 meter elephant

256 x 256 pixels

=

After converting to the size in the game...

Approximate height of a 140 centimeter child

4 x 4 meters

When a texture sheet is 256 x 256 pixels, it is 4 meters^2 in the real world.

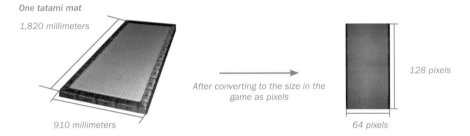

One tatami mat

1,820 millimeters

910 millimeters

After converting to the size in the game as pixels

128 pixels

64 pixels

The game in this book has a Japanese setting. The benchmark of 910 x 1,820 millimeters for one tatami mat in a Japanese-style house converts to approximately 64 x 128 pixels. We use this resolution when drawing the tatami mat texture.

We will draw a texture based on the texture resolution outline in the game specifications, while maintaining awareness of the texture's proportions.

Example when the door's texture resolution is correct

Example when the door's texture resolution is too low

When the texture resolutions all differ, the game does not look good. Where possible, try to use similar texture resolutions. Notice that only the sliding door textures are blurred.

However, a smaller texture size may be acceptable for locations the camera has difficulty seeing, or when the poor texture resolution will be unnoticed.

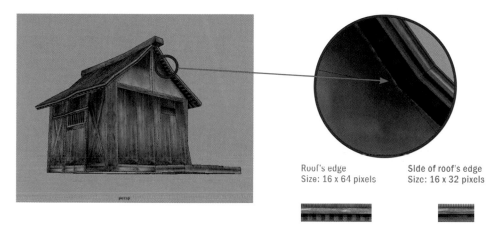

Roof's edge
Size: 16 x 64 pixels

Side of roof's edge
Size: 16 x 32 pixels

You can lower the texture size and resolution of areas the camera will not zoom-in on or notice, such as beneath the roof's edge.

With textures drawn with a simple design, such as the side of the roof, you can horizontally stretch and shrink the texture size. The camera will not notice its lower texture resolution.

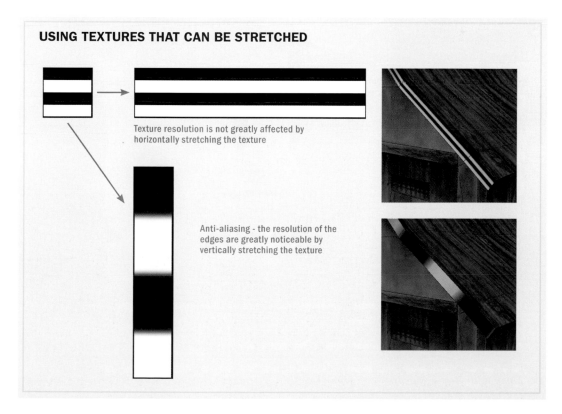

USING TEXTURES THAT CAN BE STRETCHED

Texture resolution is not greatly affected by horizontally stretching the texture

Anti-aliasing - the resolution of the edges are greatly noticeable by vertically stretching the texture

● **UV Mapping**

Texture Sheets

We briefly explained UV mapping in chapter 5, *Creating Backgrounds*. However, we will elaborate on the method in a bit more detail, using a house as an example.

The diagram below shows the completed house. Only one texture sheet was used.

Finished Model

Texture sheet size 256 X 256 pixels

Magnified

We explained before that a sheet combines numerous smaller texture images, like a jigsaw puzzle or decal sheet.

We will prepare the texture sheet here in the same way.

Now, we will breakdown this sheet to examine how the texture images are actually laid out within it.

● Division of Texture Sheets

A. Wall: 128 x 64 pixels **B.** Wall: 128 x 64 pixels **C.** Roof: 128 × 128 pixels

M. Door: 96 x 48 pixels

D. Roof ridge: 16 x 256 pixels

I. Roof's edge : 16 x 64 pixels

N. Beneath roof's edge: 16 x 48 pixels

E. Roof ridge: 16 x 256 pixels

J. Side of roof's edge : 16 x 32 pixels

O. Window: 16 x 32 pixels

F. Veranda: 48 x 128 pixels

K. Incidental plank: 16 x 32 pixels

P. Window: 32 x 64 pixels

G. Side of veranda: 8 x 128 pixels

I. Column: 16 x 128 pixels

Q. Beneath roof: 48 x 64 pixels

H. Side of veranda: 8 x 128 pixels

R. Section of roof ridge: 32 x 32 pixels

S. Doorframe: 80 x 16 pixels

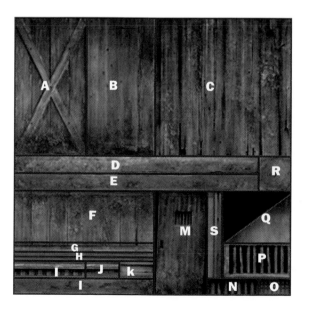

Section Three

- **UV Mapping Pipeline**

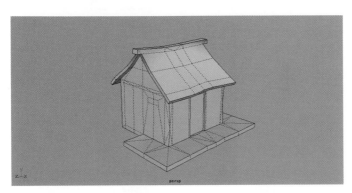

1. Prepare the model

The polygon count is 440.

2. Assign the texture to the model you will map

Texture sheet

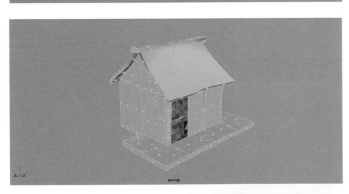

3. The house with the texture assigned

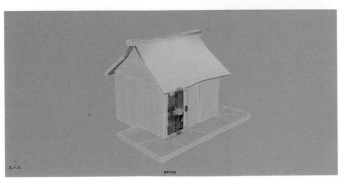

4. Create UVs for texture

Using **Polygon UVs →
Planar Mapping**, create UVs
for the texture.

Using the texture projection manipulator, move UVs to match the texture to where you want it on the choot.

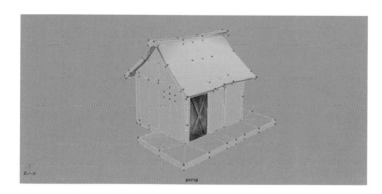

5. Apply the textures

Repeat this method, and apply the other textures that you want assigned to the sheet.

6. Completed model with textures

Diagram displaying how and where each part was UV mapped.

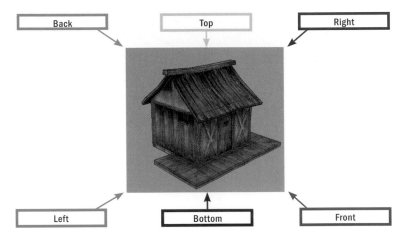

Similar to the diagrams above, we will diagram the house from six angles.

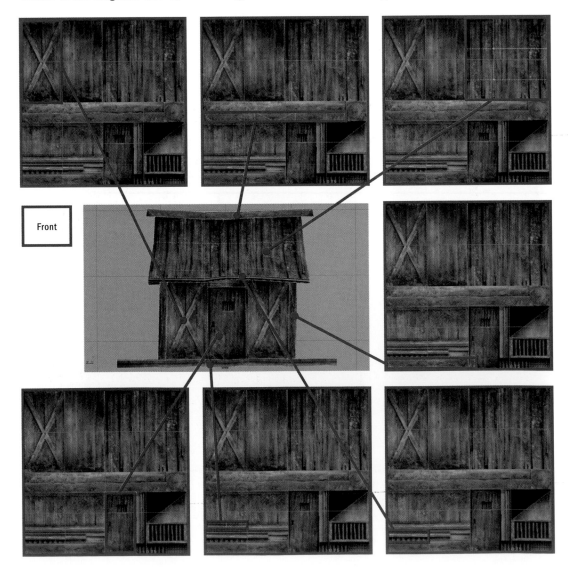

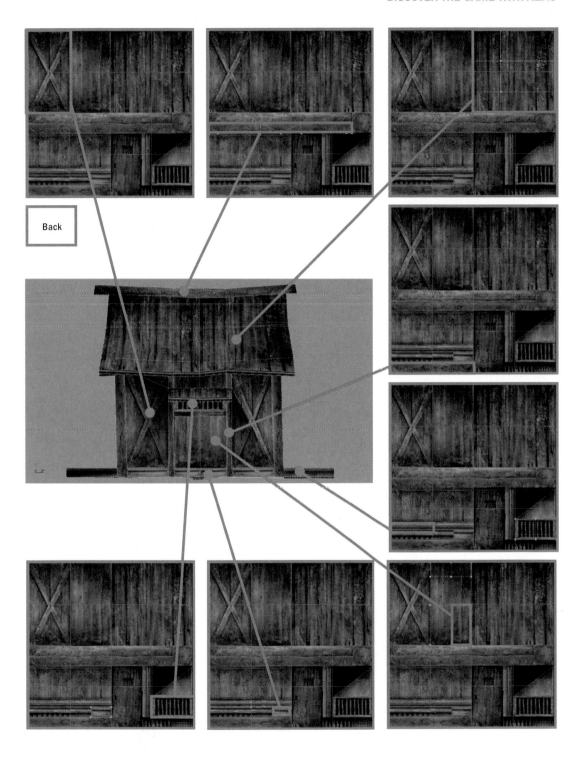

Back

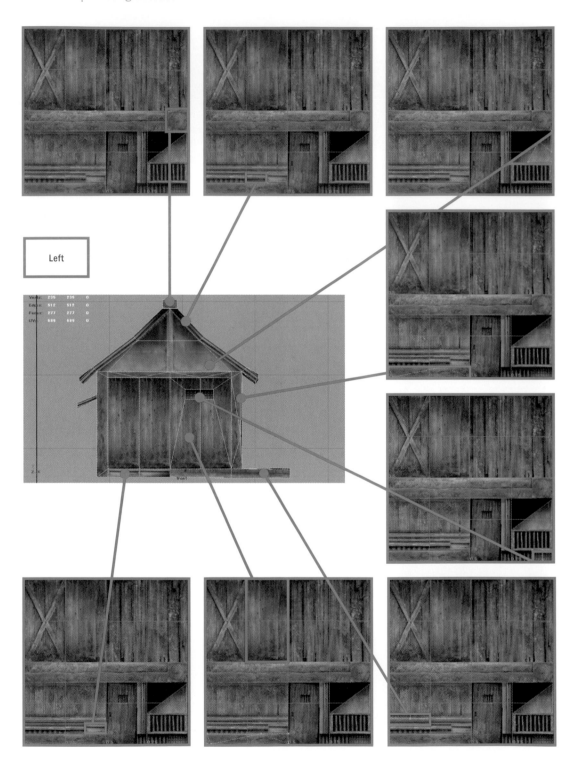

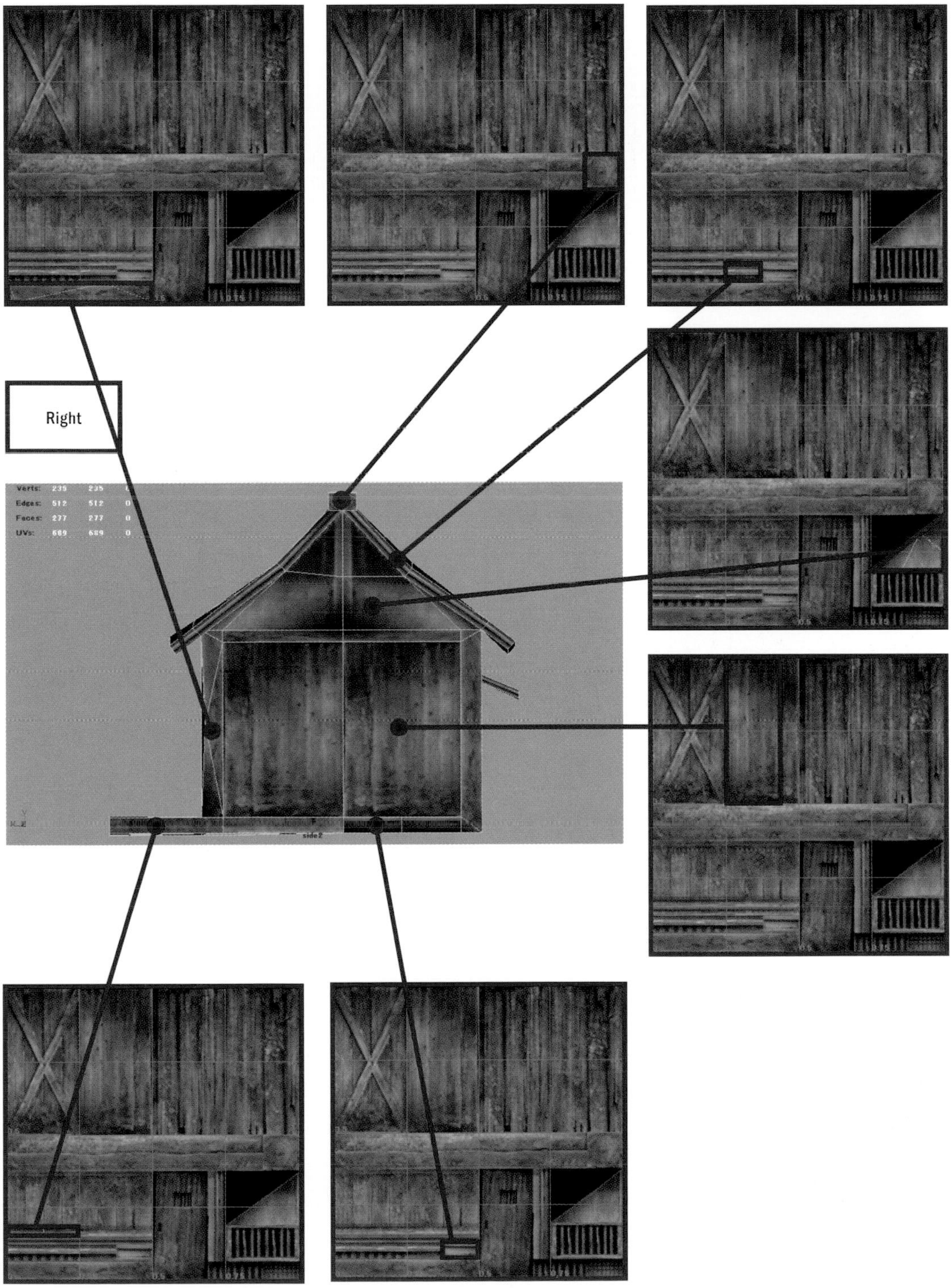

Right

Verts: 235   235   0
Edges: 512   512   0
Faces: 277   277   0
UVs: 569   609   0

side 2

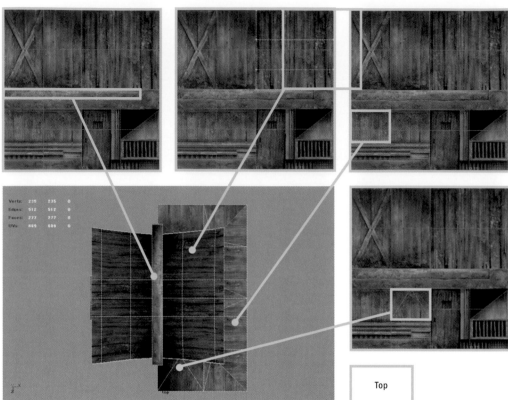

Top

Bottom

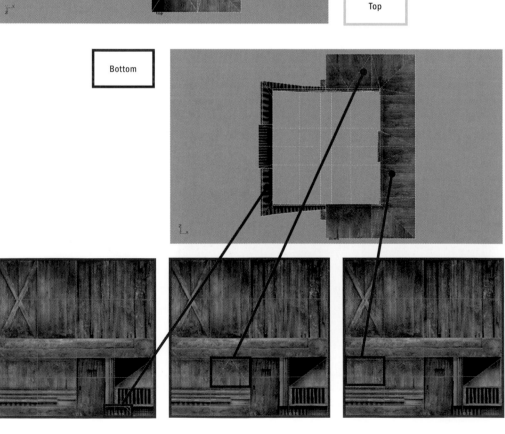

● Creating Variations

Next, we will create variations of the house model.

(**A**) to (**D**) all use the same basic house model.

The same model can look dramatically different by simply switching the textures.

As well, keeping the same texture and switching the model also significantly changes the overall impression. Variations of the house can be created with the same texture, while using some ingenuity to slightly alter the model.

● **Production Process: Create a Buried House**

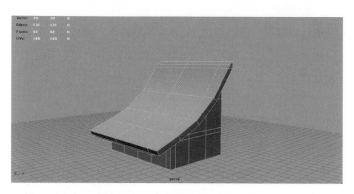

1. First, we will create 1/4 of the house by using standard polygon modeling techniques.

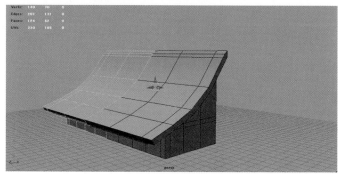

Using **Polygons** → **Mirror** → **Geometry** creates a symmetrical copy.

Additional symmetrical copies are created.

Make sure that at the time of copying, the symmetrical copies are merged into one object.

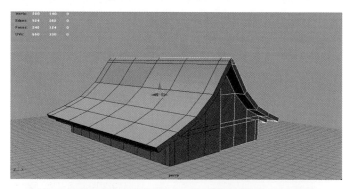

Using UV projection tools, layout UVs for the texture.

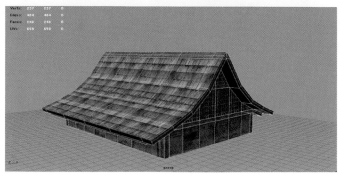

Tile the roof texture

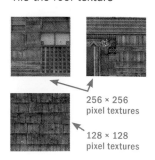

256 × 256 pixel textures

128 × 128 pixel textures

• Production Process: Improving the House

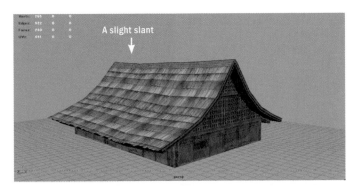

A slight slant

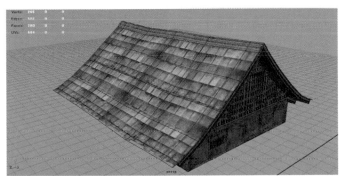

1. Transform the vertices to slant the roof towards the middle, and refine the overall shape of the house.

Try not to let the walls and pillars that hold up the house break apart too much. A slant towards the middle is enough for the house.

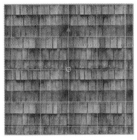

This is how the UVs look

Tile the basic roof texture twice on the UV axis.

128 x 128 pixels

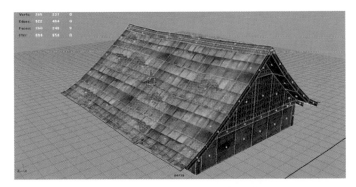

To improve the realism of the house, randomly apply textures of a broken down roof to polygon faces on the roof, without moving their UVs.

With each texture change, the impression conveyed by the roof also changes.

Tile the texture twice on the UV axis to add mood.

128 x 128 pixels

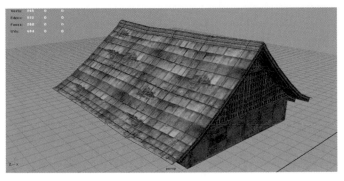

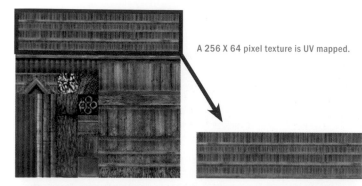

A 256 X 64 pixel texture is UV mapped.

2. Continue to refine the roof

Proceed to assign the texture that overlaps the middle of the roof's ridge.

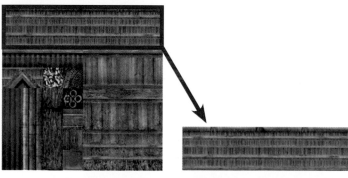

If gradual highlights are added to the over-lapping part (roof's ridge), it appears rounded over the top of the roof.

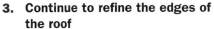

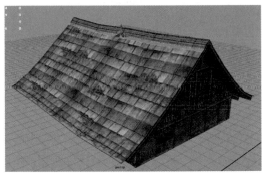

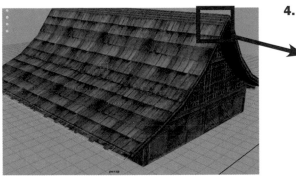

3. Continue to refine the edges of the roof

Using **Edit Polygons** → **Extrude Edge**, add polygons to the borders between the overlapping part of the roof's ridge and roof tiles/plank.

UV map these new faces to apply a texture with an alpha.

Color channel

Alpha channel

4.

The polygons do not overlap - one layer is slightly elevated over the other layer of polygons.

Side view

Texture and UVs

Color channel

Alpha channel

We will now do the same for the roof's eaves troughs.

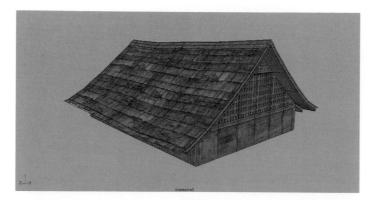

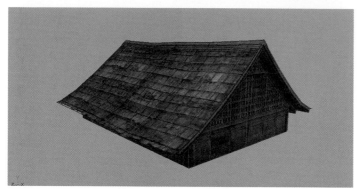

5. Adjust the model, textures, etc.

Where the house meets the ground, match its textures to the colors of the soil and foliage. Thus, making the house look naturally buried in the ground.

Using **Edit Polygons → Colors → Apply Color**, and add vertex color.

We add vertex color like the diagram above. A more detailed explanation of vertex color will be provided later in this book

6. Place the buried house on the ground

Place the house in the swamp by rotating it.

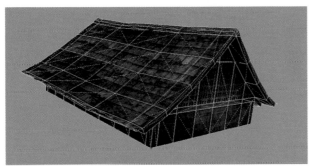

7. Place small boxes beside the house

The polygon count is 466.

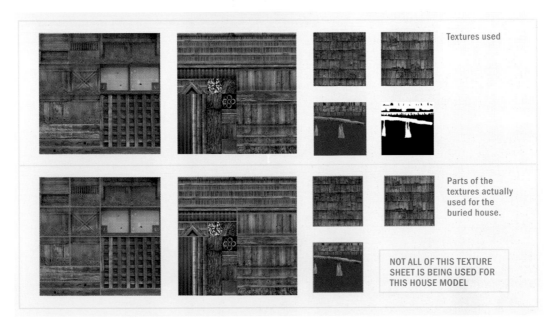

Textures used

Parts of the textures actually used for the buried house.

NOT ALL OF THIS TEXTURE SHEET IS BEING USED FOR THIS HOUSE MODEL

● Production Process: Creating the Water Mill

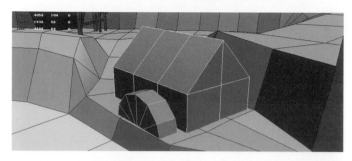

1. Continue by creating the water mill

Model the basic shape.

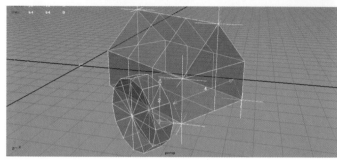

By using **Create → Measure Tools → Distance Tool**, we check the basic model's size to decide its texture size.

Then start texturing.

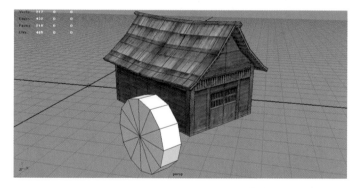

Model and layout UVs for the water mill in a manner similar to the house.

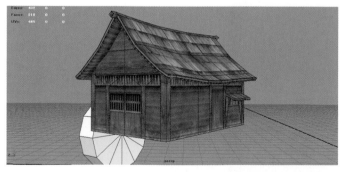

Look at it from different angles in order to assess the model.

> **Note:** *Texture size can be decided by measuring the size of the model. The same can be said of other models.*

● Production Process: Creating a Water Wheel

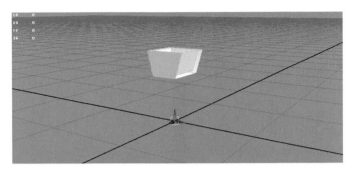

1. Start by modeling one section of the water wheel. Begin with a polygon cube and extrude faces to develop the shape.

It might be efficient to UV map at this time.

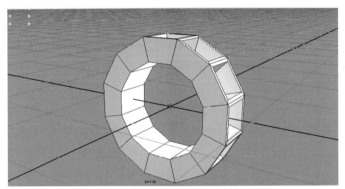

Copy the part eleven times, while rotating the object 30 degrees each time.

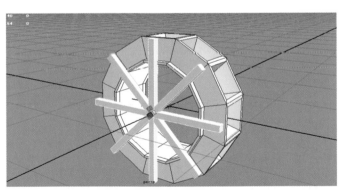

Copy the frame of the water wheel three times, while rotating it by 45 degrees each time.

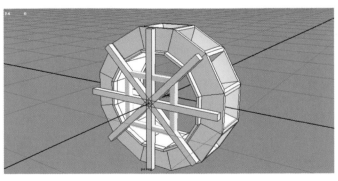

Similarly, copy the frame supports three times, while rotating them by 45 degrees each time.

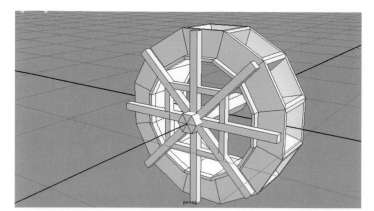

Use a polygon cylinder to create the water wheel shaft.

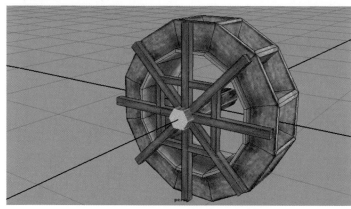

2. Use the UV Texture Editor and layout UVs for the texture.

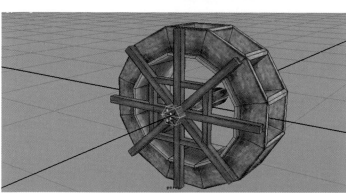

3. Re-distribute the polygons in the cross-section of the water wheel shaft by deleting edges and then re-splitting faces.

By re-distributing, we lower the cross-section's polygon count from 6 polygons to 4 polygons.

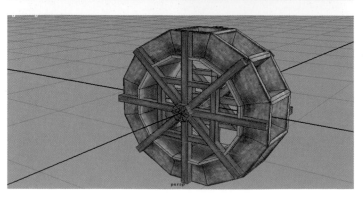

4. Symmetrically copy the frame and the frame supports for the opposite side of the water wheel (the water wheel's rear).

● Production Process: Improving the Water Wheel

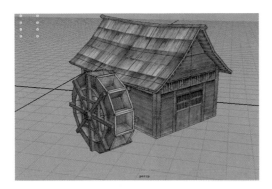

1. First, make adjustments to the water wheel texture

Next, match the color of the water wheel to that of the water mill.

We Draw details to make the wood of the water wheel look damp.

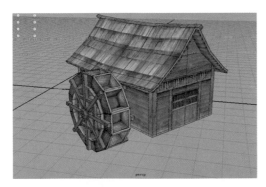

Continue to make these minor adjustments.

Draw water stains on the inside corners of the water wheel buckets.

Further improve the realism by drawing moss-like green stains.

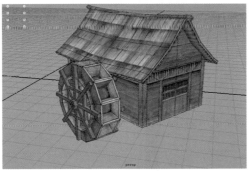

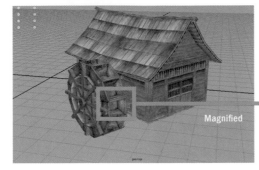

Magnified

Final texture used for the water wheel

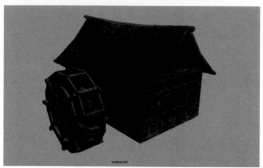

2. Additional adjustments are made, such as adding vertex color

The polygon count is 1,030.

Finish by placing the water mill on the ground beside the house.

Note: *Compared to the houses, the polygon count of the water mill is higher, due to the inclusion of the water wheel. To compensate, make adjustments by slightly reducing the polygon count of the houses.*

● Production Process: Arranging the Houses

1. Arrange all the houses on the game's level ground

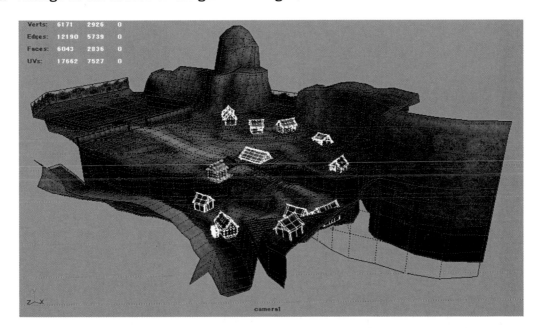

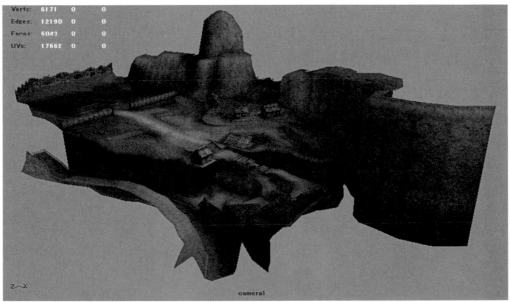

Completed model with textures.
(The total polygon count for the houses is 4,126 polygons.)

Chapter **07**

CREATING TREES

Introduction

A tree is composed of a trunk, several branches and foliage.

If we create the tree trunk and branches polygon-by-polygon, we will have a sizeable polygon count. To avoid that, we need to create the tree by cleverly using *non-transparencies*.

The non-transparencies technique will be discussed in greater detail later in this chapter.

Also keep in mind the position of the game camera and how the tree looks from that point of view. Choose the method that displays the tree best, while maintaining a low polygon count model.

Furthermore, try to conserve the polygon count whenever possible. Based on how close the background models will be to the camera, divide them into categories of *near*, *mid-range* and *distant*.

At that point, use instancing to copy and arrange the trees in order to conserve polygons.

• New Terms in This Chapter

One-sided Polygon: A polygon that only displays a texture in the direction of the face normal.

Dual-sided Polygon: A polygon that displays the textures both in the direction of the face normal and the opposite direction.

Alpha Priority: A priority order that needs to be given to the polygons with 8-bit alpha channel textures. The order is relative to a polygon's distance from the camera compared to the other polygons. In setting an alpha priority, the transparent parts are easily removed. Alpha priority will be discussed in further detail later in the chapter.

Z Sort Algorithm: An algorithm that orders the polygons, and then displays polygons with their centers farthest from the camera on-screen first.

Z Buffer Algorithm: An algorithm that orders and displays polygons on-screen by their pixel units.

Collision: This is also known as the *contact setting*. This setting determines when a character, wall, etc. makes contact in game play.

Instance Object: The object created when another object is instance copied. This instance object is a facsimile. Even if several instance objects are placed on-screen, as long as they originate from the same object they reduce the total file size. For example, a forest is often created from the instance objects of one tree object.

● **Game Camera**

The game camera movement must be considered when planning how to model.

Always consider how and what part of a model the camera will show on-screen.

The following are types of game cameras for real-time game applications:

Camera that follows the character's rear

Bird's eye camera that follows the character

Camera that is the character's point of view

Camera that rotates its view centered on the characters

When modeling, consider the camera movement in order to prevent a model's polygons from breaking apart.

• Conventional Camera Set-up

A few years ago, games did not use many polygons or textures. Instead, they commonly used the following type of model:

The model was simple, with textures applied to two polygon planes

The object viewed from above

Side view, a two-dimensional one-layer polygon

This type of model always faces in the same direction to the camera, preventing its polygons from breaking apart.

Presently, most foliage and tree models are still created this way.

● Polygon Specifications: One-sided and Dual-sided Polygons

The face normals are displayed on the outside face of a polygon. However, depending on the situation, the face normals are sometimes displayed on the polygon's other side as well.

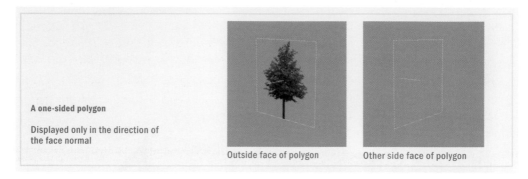

A one-sided polygon

Displayed only in the direction of the face normal

Outside face of polygon   Other side face of polygon

A dual-sided polygon

Displayed regardless of the direction of the face normal

Outside face of polygon   Other side face of polygon

When modeling with one-sided polygons, the other side may be visible. In such cases, we need to add a second polygon to hide the other side of the one-sided polygon. At such times, difficulties will arise from using the same coordinates for the second polygon. We should slightly offset the second polygon from the first one-sided polygon.

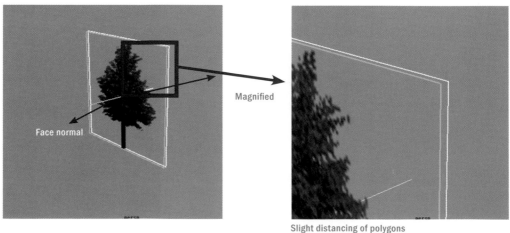

Face normal   Magnified

Slight distancing of polygons

• Texture Specifications - Alpha Priority

We already explained the two types of non-transparencies – 1-bit that overlap and 8-bit with alpha. However, we should be careful when we apply 8-bit alpha channel textures to a polygon.

Z Sort and Z Buffer algorithms are ways to display polygons with alphas. A Z Sort algorithm orders the polygons and displays the first polygon with its center farthest from the camera on-screen. A Z Buffer algorithm orders and displays the polygons on-screen by their pixel units.

Consequently, the order of the polygons from the camera becomes important. Therefore, when applying 8-bit alpha channel textures on the polygons, we need to establish an order for the polygons from the camera.This is called alpha priority.

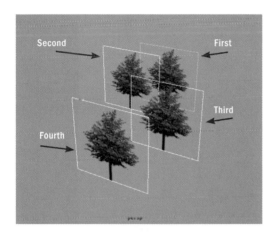

The priority order can be determined by the order of nodes, object file names and other factors. Therefore, please follow the given game specifications (1-bit & 8-bit).

It is difficult to determine the priority order when the polygons are intricately interwoven (1-bit).

In other words, we should use *1-bit overlap* non-transparencies for objects with interwoven polygons, such as trees.

In doing so, we do not need to establish an alpha priority.

● Instance Arrangement

A function called *instancing* can be used to create facsimiles, arranging several objects as though they were already created. This function reduces the time it takes a game engine to display a large quantity of objects (such as trees) on-screen.

Using this function here, we position the original tree. Instancing is achieved by using the **Instance** option in the **Edit Duplicate Tool**.

Original tree model

Instances

When anything is changed in the original tree model (used to instance copy other tree models), it will automatically update in the instance objects.

When positioning instance objects, the norm is to create the original model at X, Y, Z = (0,0,0).

Each instance object has its own coordinates. The game engine displays the object on-screen using the coordinate information.

The points of the trees are linked

- ## Models by Distance

We conserve polygons by categorizing background models as near, mid-range and distant (depending on the model's distance from the camera).

Near background model
312 polygons

Mid-range background model
14 polygons

Distant background model
2 polygons

Near background model 114 polygons

> **Note:** *Increasing the variation of the near background models by altering the position of the branches is a good idea.*

- ## Tree Modeling Tips

Depending on the game engine, we sometimes only display a texture in the direction of the face normal. For this, we should use two layers of one-sided polygons positioned together. When doing so, by using the same coordinates for the pair of one-sided polygons, we may end up merging their two textures together. We therefore need to position them slightly apart.

The use of a dual-sided polygon makes this unnecessary, and working with only one texture layer should not pose a problem. We must also set the alpha priority for 8-bit alpha textures, while it is unnecessary for 1-bit overlap textures.

In other words, we should draw *1-bit overlap non-transparent* textures for models with interwoven polygons, such as trees.

A tree will be created with dual-sided polygons. Additional trees will be arranged with instance copy.

• Arranging Models by Distance

When arranging near, mid-range and distant background models, we consider the distance from the camera.

In a game, a character cannot move beyond certain areas of the level.

Set the contact setting, or collision, to designate the locations inaccessible to the game characters.

Set the locations of such structures as the house walls, fences and rock walls.

A game program often incorporates the change of level sections and loading (program-reading) points into its collision settings.

Loading Point

Collision

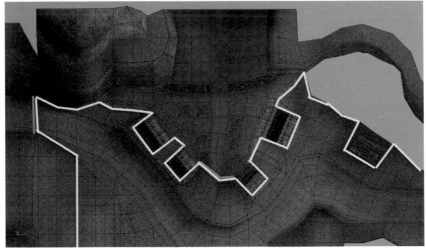

Top view of a section of the background map

Perspective view of a section of the background map

Place the trees within these collision and loading point boundaries.

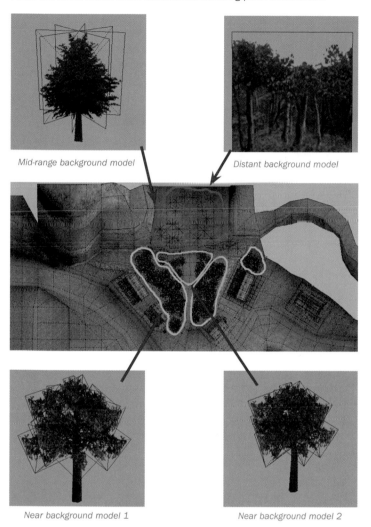

Mid-range background model

Distant background model

Near background model 1

Near background model 2

Place near background
models in locations
unaffected by collisions.

Image placed with background models

Tree Modeling: Fractal Composition

A tree branch gradually becomes more intricate as it extends away from the tree trunk. The branch also sub-divides several times into increasingly smaller branches. It sub-divides with accelerating frequency as it extends away from the tree trunk.

Overview of the tree

When we look at a section of a living thing (such as a branch on a tree), it may appear to be a miniaturized version of the living thing.

This is called *fractal composition.*

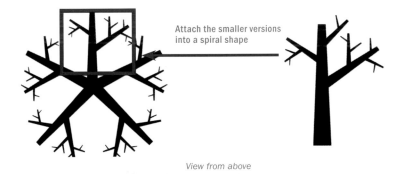

Attach the smaller versions into a spiral shape

View from above

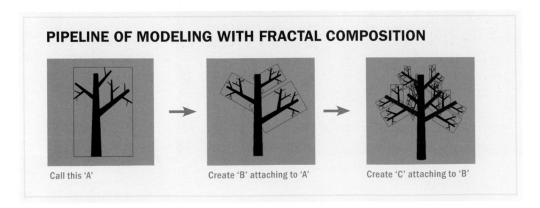

PIPELINE OF MODELING WITH FRACTAL COMPOSITION

Call this 'A'   Create 'B' attaching to 'A'   Create 'C' attaching to 'B'

● Tree Texture: Texture Background

Based on the tree's composition, create the textures for the larger and smaller branches.

Larger branch   *Smaller branch*

Create the textures with non-transparencies, but use one color for the sheet's backdrop. In doing so, we smooth the texture edges after removing the transparencies.

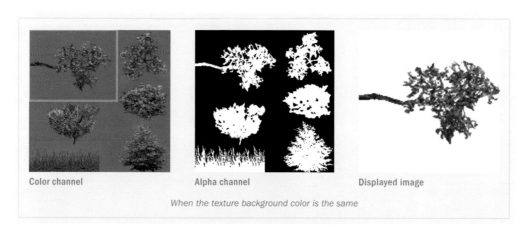

Color channel   Alpha channel   Displayed image

When the texture background color is the same

If anti-aliased, the black in the background will overlap into the edges.

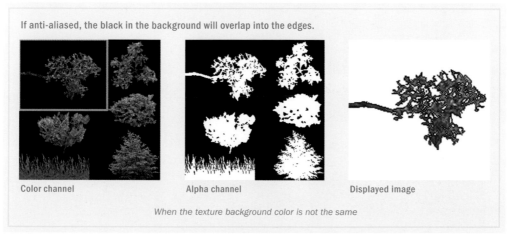

Color channel   Alpha channel   Displayed image

When the texture background color is not the same

● **Production Process: Create Near Background Models**

Create a Tree Trunk

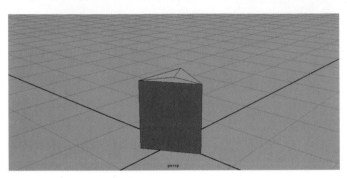

1. We will now create the near (or close proximity) background models.

First, create a three-sided cylinder.

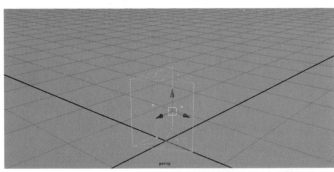

Erase the excess polygon faces at the top and bottom of the cylinder.

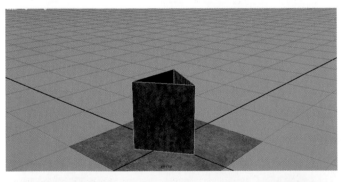

Layout UVs for the texture.

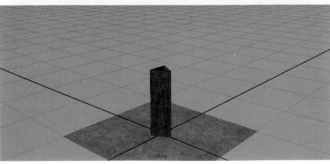

Refine the size of the tree trunk.

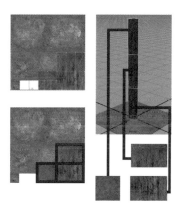

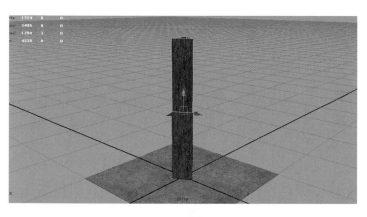

Similarly, create the second part of the tree trunk. With the third part, cap off the top polygon.

UV map the three cylinders stacked on each other, and merge them into one object.

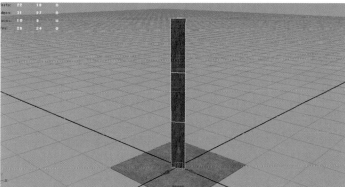

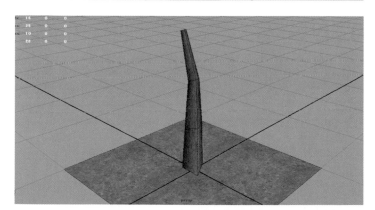

These are the tree trunk UVs. The third part's texture is small, because the third part is not very noticeable.

2. Continue to refine the shape of the tree trunk.

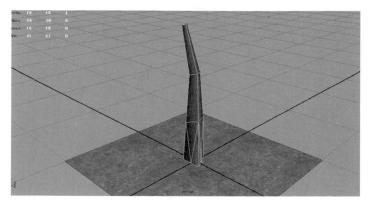

Subdivide the polygons at the base of the tree trunk to create triangular polygon faces.

175

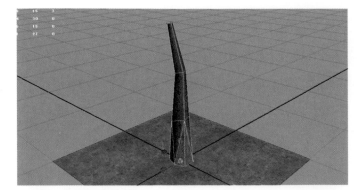

By moving the vertices, we round the base of the tree trunk.

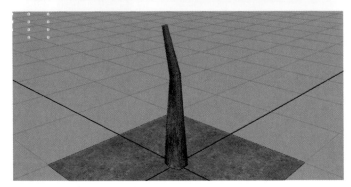

● Create the Higher Branches

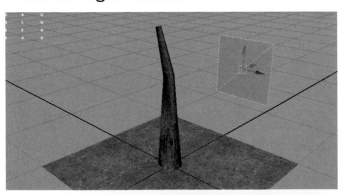

1. Create a single polygon plane for a branch.

Layout UVs for the texture.

Color and alpha channels

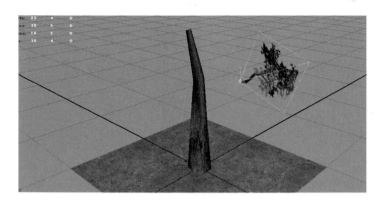

Rotate the polygon and move the pivot to the root of the branch.

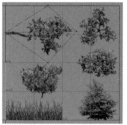

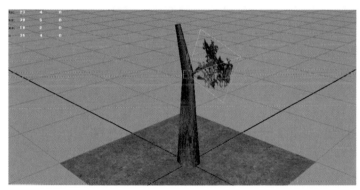

Roughly position the branch on the tree trunk.

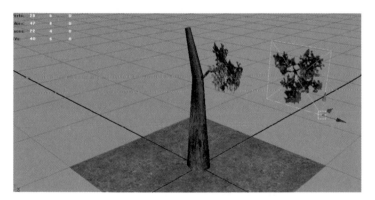

Next, create an even smaller branch by creating a new single polygon plane and laying out UV's.

Position the final branch on the tree trunk.

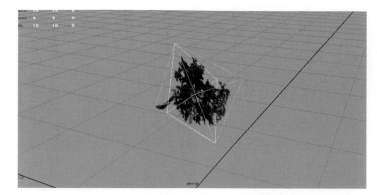

2. As it is now when viewed from the side, the appearance of the branch has no dimension to it.

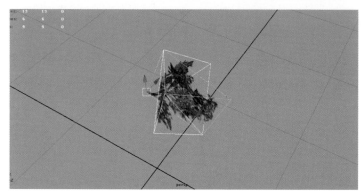

To add dimension, slightly indent the point at the center, like a parabolic antenna.

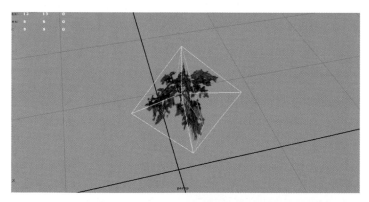

Changing its shape, the branch has dimension from any angle.

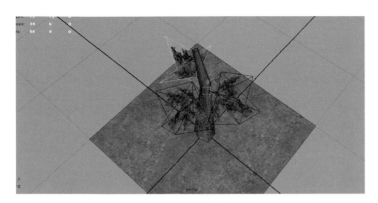

3. Arrange the completed branches to extend in all directions from the tree trunk.

Place the branches with their ends tilted slightly up.

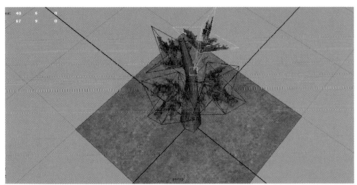

This is the final tree model.

To get a better idea of the tree, hide the polygon outline.

● Create the Lower Branches

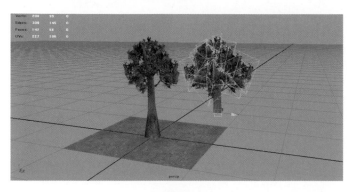

1. Shorten the tree by copying everything except the bottom part of the trunk.

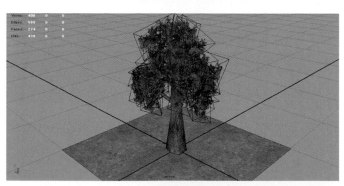

Arrange the branches on the lower trunk to extend in all directions from the tree trunk.

Work your way down the tree.

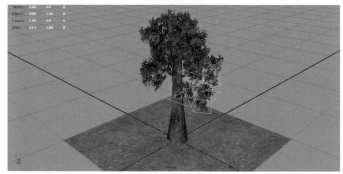

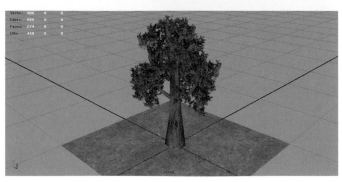

2. Gradually refine the shape of the tree.

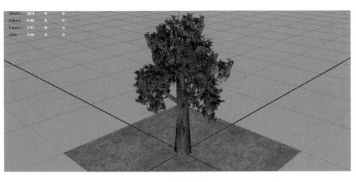

To ensure that the composition is correct, we make adjustments to the tree while rotating it by 360 degrees.

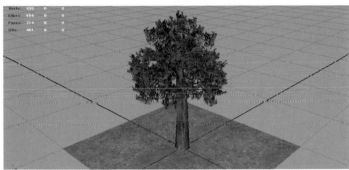

Attach more intricate branches to the lower part of the tree, where the camera zooms-in. Attach the more simple branches to the upper part, where the camera will not be able to zoom-in. This way, we can efficiently distribute the tree's polygon count.

3. After adding vertex color, the tree is complete.

With vertex color, the base of the tree trunk should be darker, while the ends of the branches should be brighter.

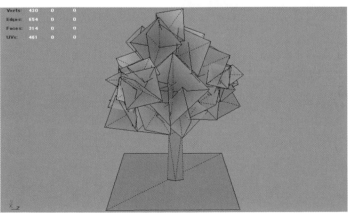

Production Process: Create Mid-range Background Trees

Create a Tree Trunk

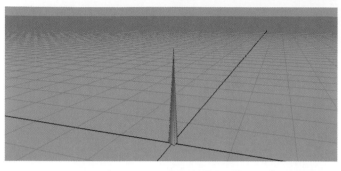

1. We will now create a mid-range background model.

First, create a three-sided polygon cone.

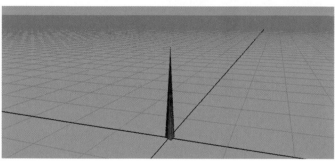

Layout the UVs.

Create Branches

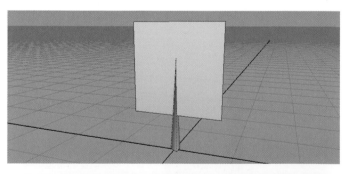

1. Create a single face polygon plane.

Place it high on the trunk.

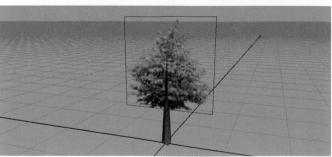

Layout the UVs.

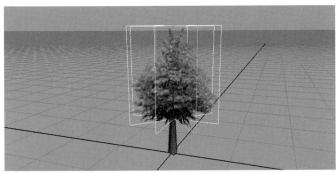

Rotate it by 45 degrees and copy the polygon twice.

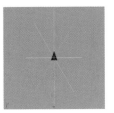

The top view

The vertex color at the ends of the branches should be set slightly brighter.

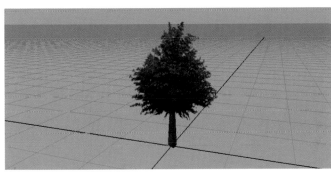

2. After adding vertex color, the tree is complete.

● Production Process: Create in the Distant Background Trees

Tile the UVs of flat polygon planes for the distant background.

The polygons are not interwoven into each other, and we can even use 8-bit alpha channels.

Color and alpha channels

Section Three

● **Tree Branch Textures**

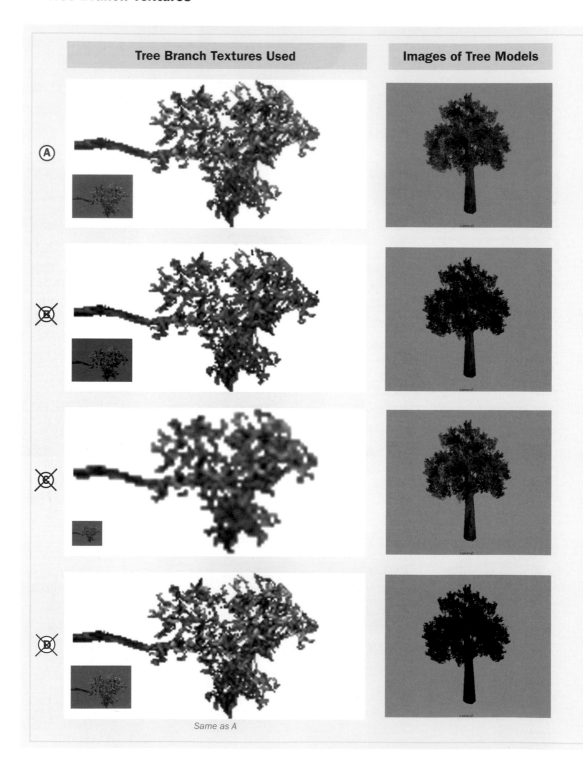

Tree Branch Textures Used | Images of Tree Models

Same as A

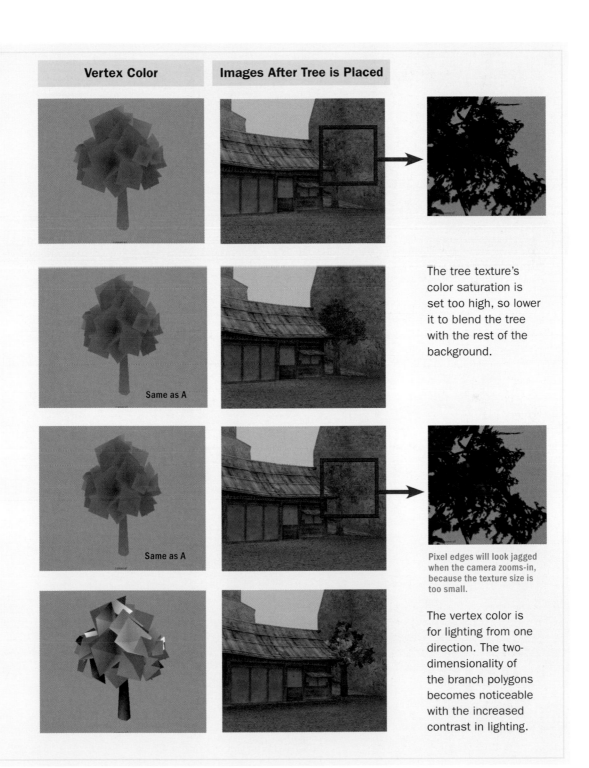

Vertex Color	Images After Tree is Placed

The tree texture's color saturation is set too high, so lower it to blend the tree with the rest of the background.

Same as A

Same as A

Pixel edges will look jagged when the camera zooms-in, because the texture size is too small.

The vertex color is for lighting from one direction. The two-dimensionality of the branch polygons becomes noticeable with the increased contrast in lighting.

Chapter **08**

CREATE FOLIAGE AND ROCKS

Introduction

Remembering the explanation given for tree creation, we can create the foliage by using 1-bit non-transparencies. Remember to create the rocks while checking their UVs, so their textures do not stretch.

One key rule is to gather and carefully study the source materials of anything equivalent in the natural world. Our goal is low-poly objects that look impressive.

There is not any one method for creating living things. We encourage you to try various methods.

Please understand that those mentioned in this book are only examples.

● Gather Source Materials

In game production, we gather as many reference source materials as possible.

Reference source materials

• Production Process: Creating Foliage 1

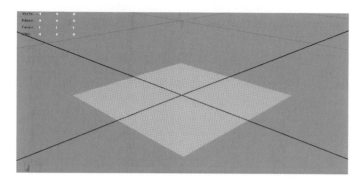

1. Create a single face polygon plane and divide the polygon into four pieces.

256 × 256 pixel textures used

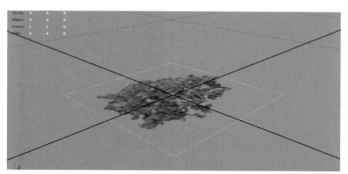

Layout the UVs

Raise the vertex at the center.

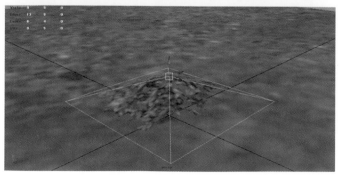

Rotate the foliage.

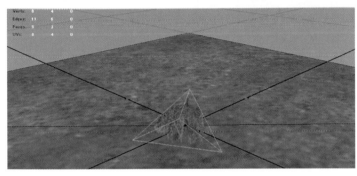

2. Create a triangular polygon plane and layout UVs.

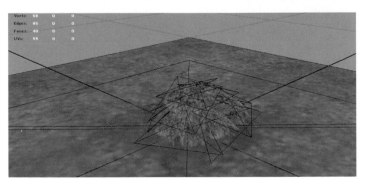

3. Place the foliage.

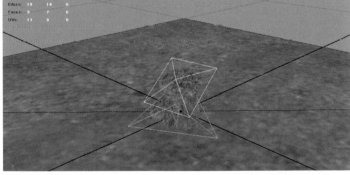

Randomly place the foliage, as shown in the diagram to the left.

4. Make adjustments to match the texture color to the background map.

The bush is complete.

It is 36 polygons.

5. Use instance copy to arrange the bushes.

6. The completed model with textures.

Finished Image

● Production Process: Creating Foliage 2

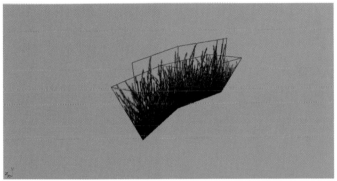

1. Create the foliage, by modeling it, following the diagram to the left.

256 × 256 pixel textures used

Layout UVs

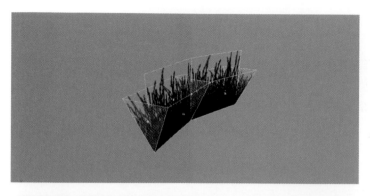

Add a triangular polygon to convey more dimensionality in the side view of the foliage.

2. The foliage is complete.

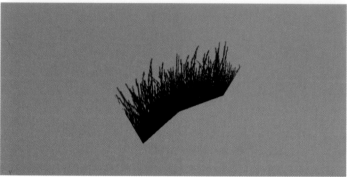

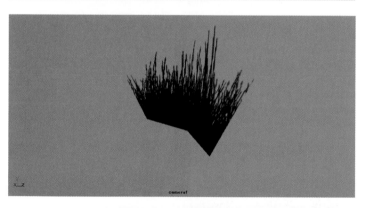

Look at it from a different angle.

3. The foliage is 19 polygons.

192

4. Layout the foliage using instanced copies.

5. The completed model with textures.

Production Process: Creating Flowers (Hydrangea)

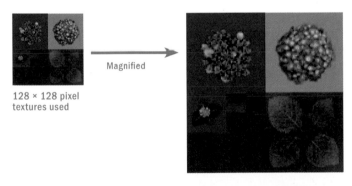

Magnified

128 × 128 pixel textures used

Create three variations of hydrangeas with these textures.

1. The hydrangea is 38 polygons.

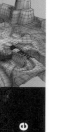

2. The hydrangea is 32 polygons.

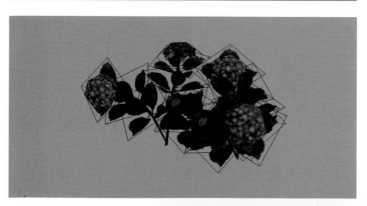

3. The hydrangea is 32 polygons.

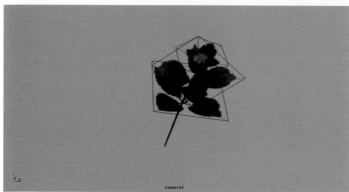

4. Arrange the various hydrangeas together.

The hydrangeas are complete.

Completed model with textures

● Production Process: Creating Rocks 1

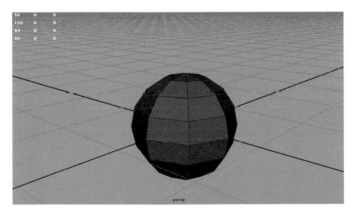

1. Create a primitive model of a sphere.

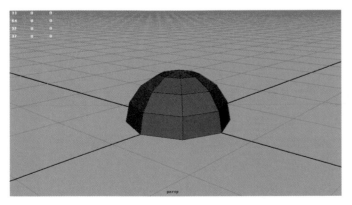

Delete the bottom half of the sphere.

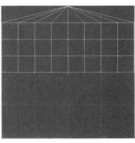

UV layout

195

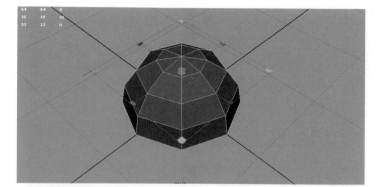

2. View the half-sphere from the top view and layout the UV.

UV layout

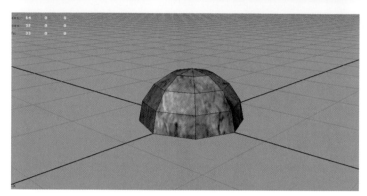

We even out the distribution of the UV and map the texture.

UV layout

128 x 128 pixels texture used

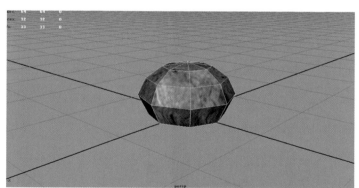

3. Scale in the points at the bottom of the rock.

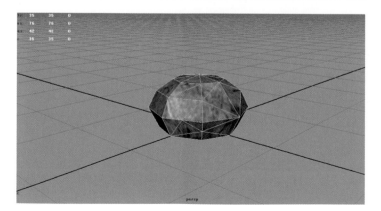

Split some faces to add polygonal triangles to make the rock look natural.

Continue to refine the shape by deleting vertices and polygon edges.

After the adjustments, the rock should be shaped as shown in the diagram to the left.

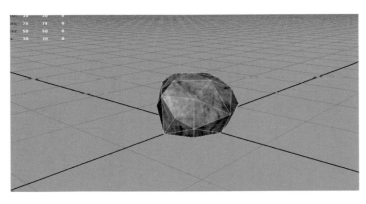

Refine the rock's shape by slightly shifting its vertices.

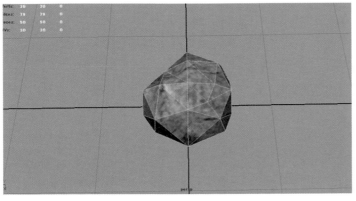

Refine the rock's shape while checking it from all angles.

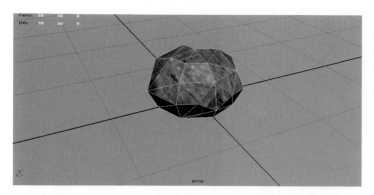

4. Re-shape the rock while preventing the texture from stretching.

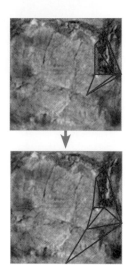

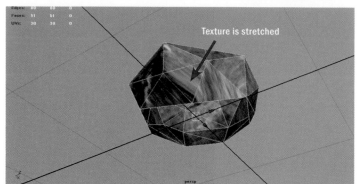

Texture is stretched

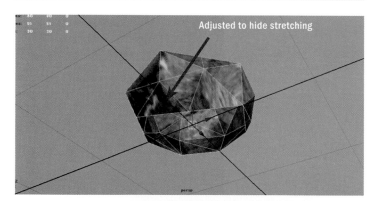

Adjusted to hide stretching

Adjust the UV to hide the stretching of the texture.

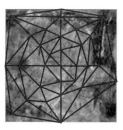

5. If left unchanged, the polygon edges are very noticeable.

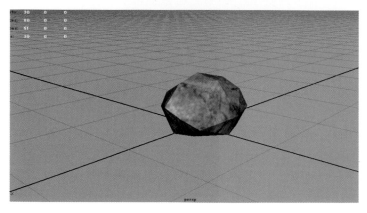

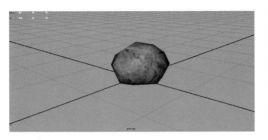

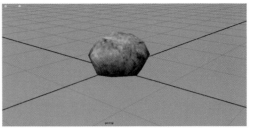

Use **Edit Polygons** → **Normals** → **Soften/ Harden** to smooth-shade the rock.

6. Finish by adding vertex color.

● Improving the Rock Texture

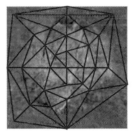

Fix the rock texture.

The rock should be drawn so it looks natural on the ground.

The rock is 52 polygons.

Completed model with textures.

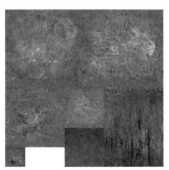

256 x 256 texture sheet used

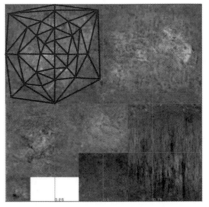

UV looks like the diagram above

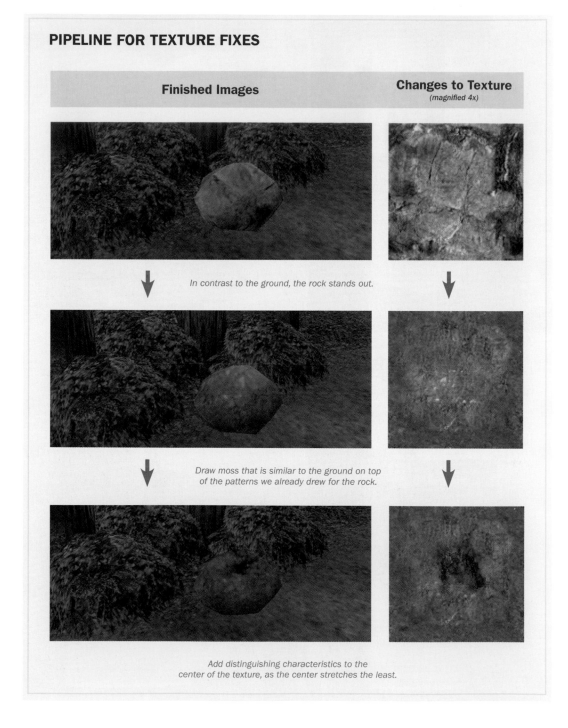

PIPELINE FOR TEXTURE FIXES

Finished Images	Changes to Texture (magnified 4x)

In contrast to the ground, the rock stands out.

Draw moss that is similar to the ground on top of the patterns we already drew for the rock.

Add distinguishing characteristics to the center of the texture, as the center stretches the least.

• Production Process: Creating Rocks 2

We further increase the variety of rock texture patterns.

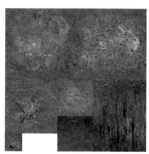

256 X 256 pixel texture used

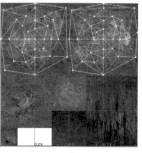

The UVs of the large rocks (1 and 2)

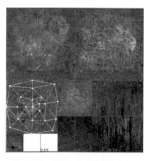

The UVs of the mid-sized rock

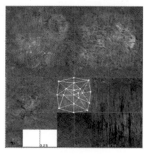

The UVs of the small rock

The UV of the rock that will be placed on top of a roof.

From the left of the diagram:

Large rock 1: 52 polygons
Large rock 2: 52 polygons
Mid-sized rock: 33 polygons
Small rock: 27 polygons
Rock that will be placed on top of a roof:
27 polygons

The rock that goes on top of a roof has a small texture size, because the camera will not zoom-in on it.

The rocks with vertex color.

Finished Images

Chapter **09**

CREATING THE STEPS & SACRED GATE

Introduction

We will create the stone steps while being aware of the weathered corners and the indented and elevated shape of the stones. Where possible, create the textures so that the straight lines of the polygons are carefully hidden.

At the base of the sacred gate's columns, create a weathered look for the wood and the dust from the ground.

● Gather Source Materials

Before creating the textures, gather and carefully examine the gradations in our source materials on the corners of the steps and base of the columns.

Source materials

● Actual Color Difference

The actual texture colors will not necessarily appear identical on-screen (on a TV monitor). The color contrast is often higher on-screen, and subtle color differences may not be visible.

Adjust the texture while periodically checking its colors on-screen.

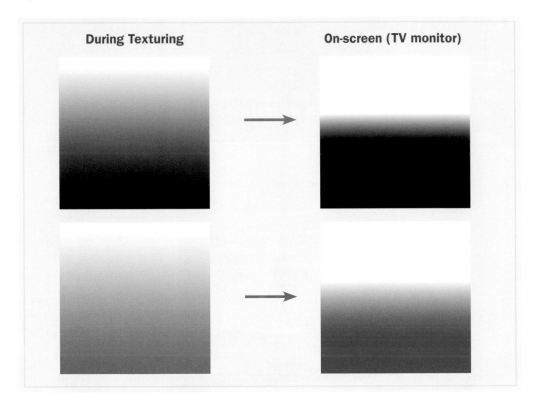

How a texture appears also varies with the type of TV. Within the industry, it is common for game developers to set-up and use only one TV monitor for all game color adjustments.

● Production Process: Creating the Sacred Gate

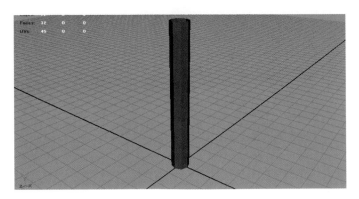

1. Create a polygon cylinder.

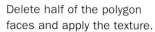

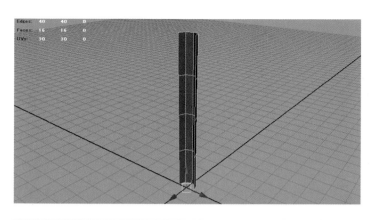

Delete half of the polygon faces and apply the texture.

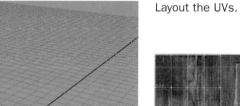

256 x 256 pixel texture used

Layout the UVs.

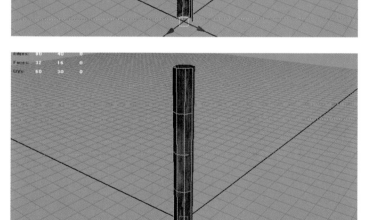

Duplicate the pillar model and rotate it 180 degrees.

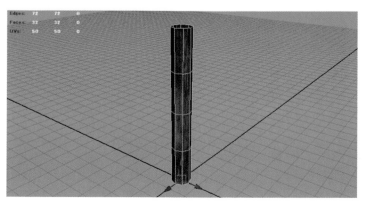

Merge the two halves to make them one object.

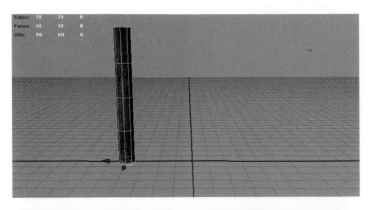

2. Move the object. To improve the quality of our work, we instance copy the pillar on the opposite side.

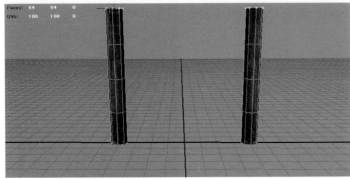

If a vertex of one pillar is selected, we see that the vertices are linked in this way between the two pillars.

Using instances, we can more easily control the overall shape of the sacred gate.

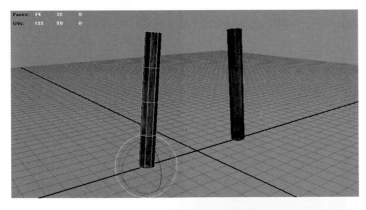

Rotate the pillars to tilt them towards each other.

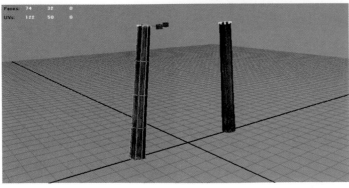

The pillars intersect in the ground when tilted. Therefore, we flatten the vertices at the base of all pillars in relation to the ground.

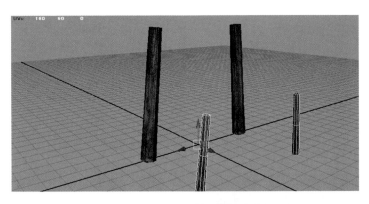

3. Most parts of the sacred gate are created in a similar way.

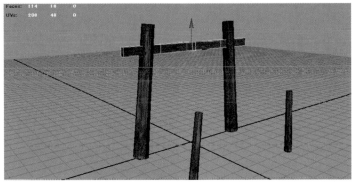

Create the horizontal beam.

Also create the front part of the sacred gate.

Add the roof. When modeling the sacred gate is almost finished, start refining its shape.

Overall, the composition of the model is weak and will need to be refined.

4. Adjust the position of the small pillars at the front.

Improve the details of the sacred gate, such as adding tilt to the pillars at their sides, and refining the shape of the roof.

Alias Tip: *Use dual monitors! You need to have the extra real estate and now that most cards have dual output, it's a must.*

David Lau | Senior Support Product Specialist

● **Production Process: Texturing the Sacred Gate**

1. Modify the texture.

Create the appearance of sand on the texture bordering the ground.

2. Attach pedestals to the bottom of the sacred gate.

Create the appearance of sand on the textures bordering the ground.

Create an impression of a shadow where the wood appears to degrade at the pedestals.

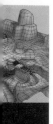

3. To create an impression of a shadow, modify the texture to lower the brightness slightly.

4. To make the sacred gate appear not newly built, modify the texture to create dirt stains and shadows on it.

Refine the balance between the pedestals.

5. Further refine the shadows.

Even through vertex coloring, the shadows do not fall on these *areas without polygons*. Therefore, we should draw shadows into the textures

Draw a shadow into the texture

In order to conserve the polygon count, you should draw as many details into the texture as you can. However, it is unnecessary when the polygons are distributed like this model.

● **Production Process: Final Adjustments**

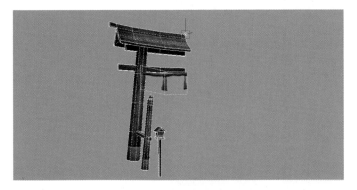

1. After most of the sacred gate is completed, delete the half that is the instance copy.

The instance copy was used to improve the quality of our work.

Keeping the instance copy, the vertex color of the left and right sides becomes identical. Moreover, we are unable to direct the paths of the shadows.

Using **Polygons→Mirror Geometry**, symmetrically copy the remaining half to create the other side of the sacred gate.

Within the mirror geometry options, merge the halves into one object.

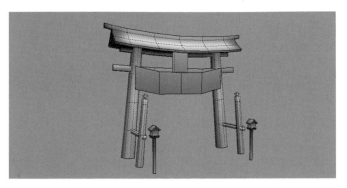

Add vertex color.

2. Adjust the overall shape of the sacred gate again.

Slightly tilt the left and right sides, as instances are no longer used.

To make the sacred gate appear naturally placed, we adjust the ground's vertex color.

The ground's polygons are laid out like the diagram to the left.

Split the ground polygons directly beneath the pillars, and add shadows with vertex color.

Complete the sacred gate with its shadow falling on the ground. Its total polygon count is 820 polygons.

• Production Process: Polygon Reduction

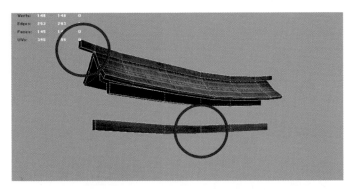

1. To conserve the polygon count, delete the polygon edges that do not greatly affect the overall shape, and redistribute the rest.

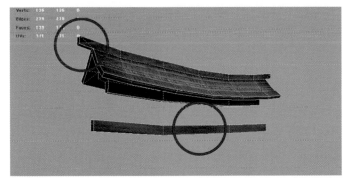

2. Take a close up look at the polygons.

This sort of low-key effort reduces the overall polygon count.

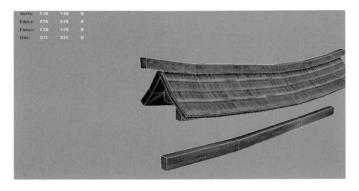

3. The total polygon count becomes 792 polygons.

We conserved 28 polygons.

Finished Images

● Production Process: Creating Rock Steps

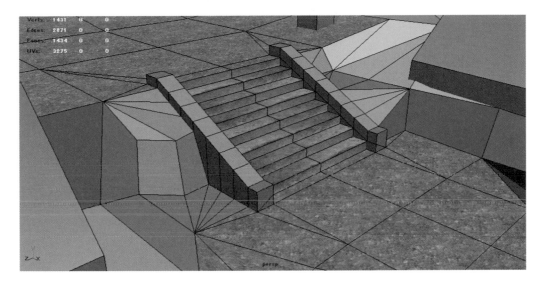

1. Follow the height difference game specifications to create the steps. In other words, model the steps with the height difference of 25 centimeters and depth of 50 centimeters.

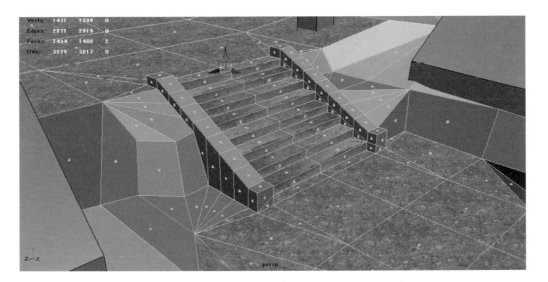

Apply basic textures, then adjust the textures.

● Production Process: Texturing Stone Steps

1. First, adjust the border of the highest step to be level with the ground.

Modify the texture to draw sand covering the step texture, and re-apply it.

The highest step now blends naturally with the ground.

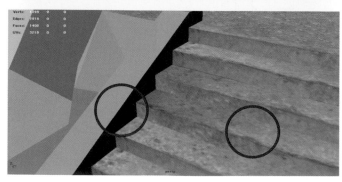

2. Next adjust the corners of the steps.

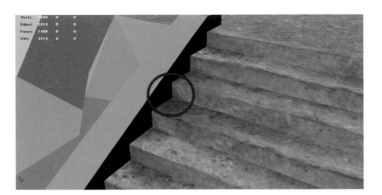

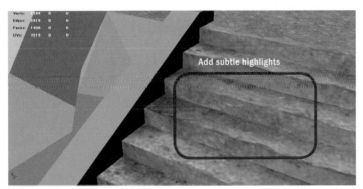

Modify the texture to draw the dirt blown into the corners. Next, adjust the polygon edges of the steps.

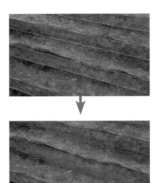

Even though they are straight lines, make the polygon edges look uneven by adding highlights to the texture. (refer to the above diagrams.)

3. To create dimension, add a few highlights to the handrails. Also add shadow and dirt to the front of each step's texture.

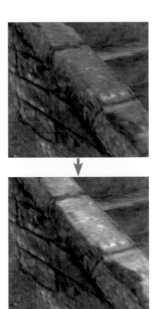

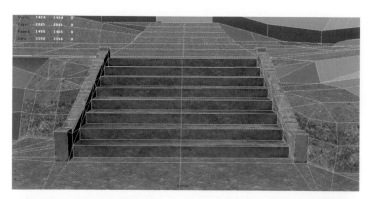

4. Move the vertices slightly to intentionally make the steps look more irregular.

Indent the middle of each step slightly, where most people would walk.

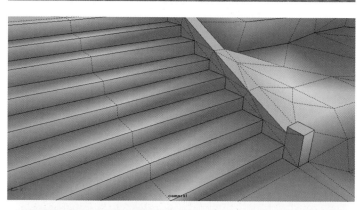

5. Add vertex color.

Lower the brightness levels in the corners.

The completed model with textures.

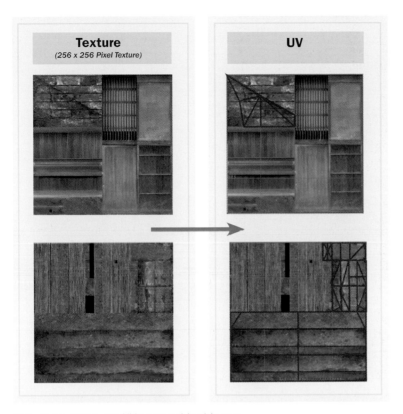

The stone steps are UV mapped in this way.

Finished Image

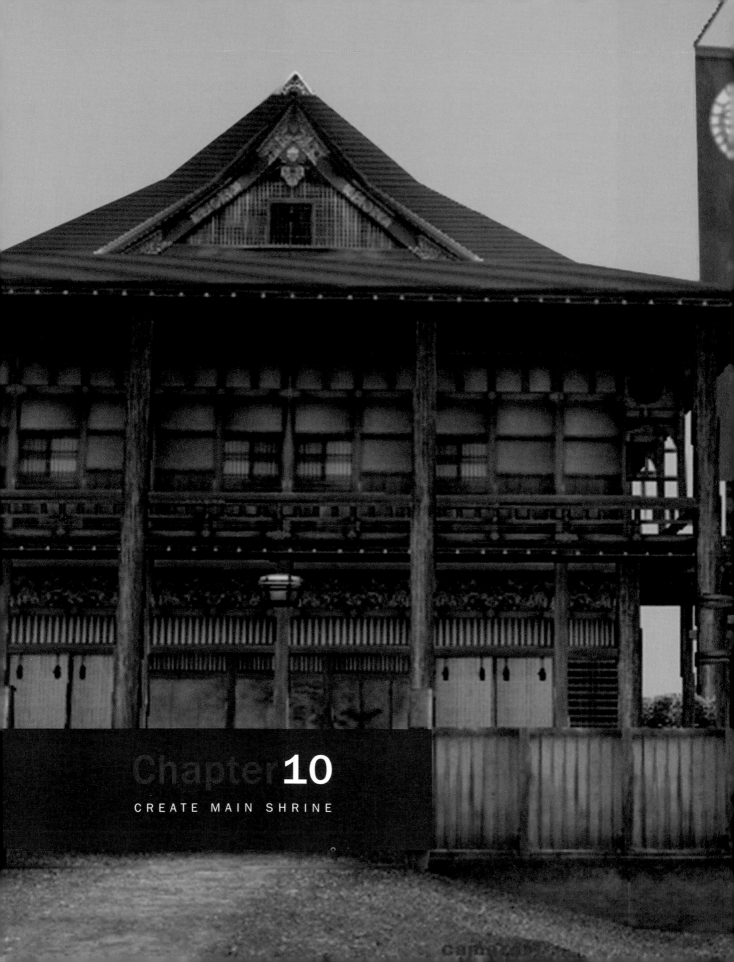

Chapter **10**

CREATE MAIN SHRINE

Introduction

Certain factors must be considered when determining an object's distance from the game loading points (where the game loads the next part of the level). Such factors include the texture size and whether to model with flat or solid polygons.

For buildings that are similar on both sides, we will first create one of the halves, and then use instance copy to create the other half. This will improve the quality of the sacred gate. We will also conserve the polygon count when the columns are instance copied.

We will apply what we learned in the previous chapters to our work here.

● Match Models and Textures to Camera Distance

The trees were laid out with their distance from the camera in mind as near, mid-range and distant level models.

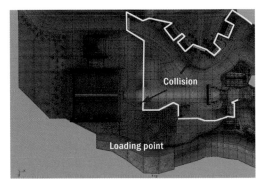

The top view of the level map

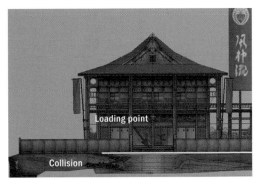

The side view of the level map

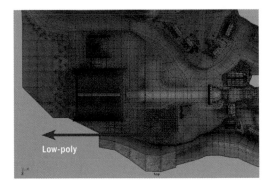

When modeling buildings, keep in mind their distances from the camera.

The model's texture resolution decreases relative to its distance from the camera.

• Flat and Solid Models

We will now look at how an object's polygon count actually changes with its distance from the camera.

First, we compare the first and second floors.

Notice that the first floor, near the camera, is composed of solid polygons, while the second floor, distant from the camera, is composed of flat polygons.

Walls, columns, beams and everything on the second floor are made from (two-dimensional) flat polygons.

Second floor magnified

Diagram of entire shrine

Walls, columns, beams and everything on the first floor are made from (three-dimensional) solid polygons.

First floor magnified

We now turn our attention to the columns. Six of them are set-up near the camera, while three columns are set-up away from it.

The distant columns are three sided cylinders

The near columns are six-sided cylinders

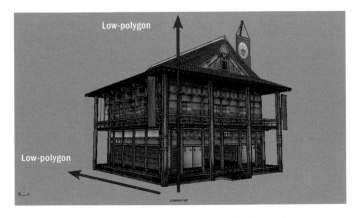

Differentiate how to model depending on the distance from the camera in these two directions.

● Change Texture Size

Look at how an object's texture size changes with its distance from the camera.

Then compare the textures of the first and second floors, as we did with the models.

We see that a regular-size texture has been applied to the first floor, near the camera, while a smaller-size texture has been applied to the second floor, distant from the camera.

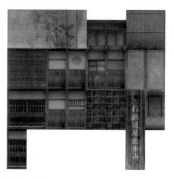

256 x 256 pixel texture used

UV layout
Wall texture size
64 x 64 pixel for one square meter

Second floor magnified

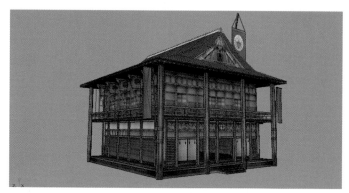

Diagram of entire shrine

256 x 256 pixel texture used

UV layout
Wall texture size
128 x 128 pixel for one square meter

First floor magnified

• Polygons with Text

For a texture with text or graphics clearly embedded in it, we should not be concerned about the texture's distance from the camera. We set an adequate texture size for the texture to always appear clearly.

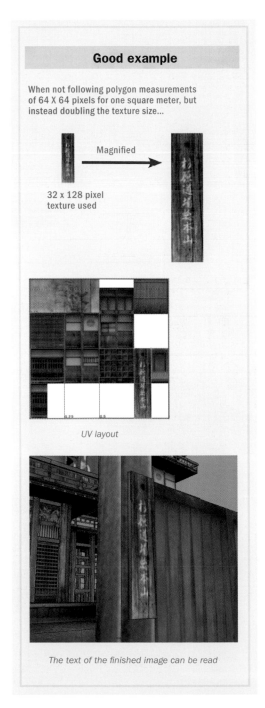

Good example

When not following polygon measurements of 64 X 64 pixels for one square meter, but instead doubling the texture size...

Magnified

32 x 128 pixel texture used

UV layout

The text of the finished image can be read

Bad example

When following polygon measurements of 64 X 64 pixels for one square meter...

Magnified

16 x 64 pixel texture used

The text of the finished image cannot be read

● Hidden Polygons

The parts distant from the camera were modelled as low-polygons.

Some parts are also hidden from the camera. Delete these unnecessary polygon faces.

Front view of the column

Rear of the
column does not
have polygons

Rear view of the column

Rear view of the entire shrine

Rear of the fence post
does not have polygons

Rear view of the fence post

Front view of the fence post

● Dual-sided Polygons

The polygon specifications in this book allow dual-sided polygons. We can therefore model parts like walls and fences with one polygon layer each.

However, we need to create the walls and fences by combining two polygon layers in some locations.

These locations have different lighting for the front and back (such as indoors and outdoors), or have different textures on the front and back.

Plank texture for the outdoor walls

Dirt texture for the indoor walls

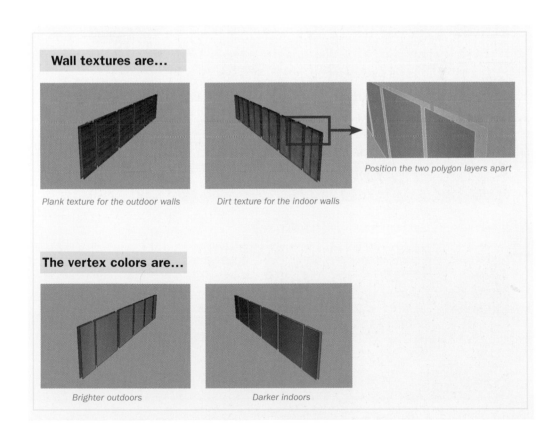

Wall textures are...

Plank texture for the outdoor walls

Dirt texture for the indoor walls

Position the two polygon layers apart

The vertex colors are...

Brighter outdoors

Darker indoors

Section Three

● **Production Process: Creating the Main Shrine**

Continue to work while keeping in mind everything we learned in previous sections.

Here we'll use instanced copies for the numerous columns, etc.

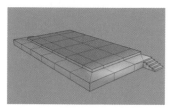  

1. Starting with a polygon primitive cube and modeling using the various polygon creation and editing tools in Maya, create half the ground floor.

Use **Polygon → Mirror Geometry** to copy the other half, and merge the two halves together into one object.

Layout UVs.

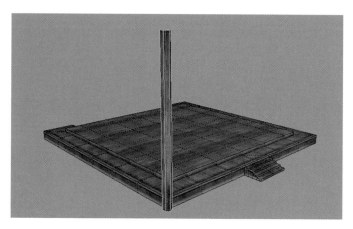 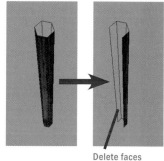

Delete faces

Delete the polygons on the back side of the column.

2. Create one column from a six-sided cylinder.

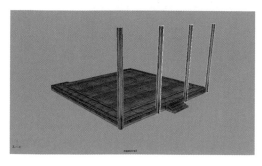 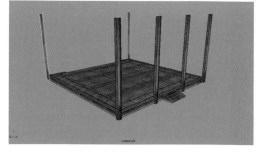

Place instanced copies of the column along the ground floor.

Create the distant column with a three-sided cylinder, and instance copy it.

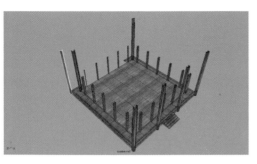

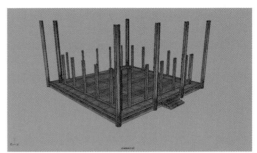

Create the other interior columns in a similar way.

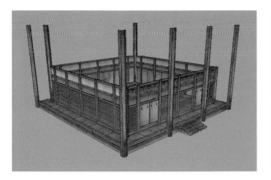

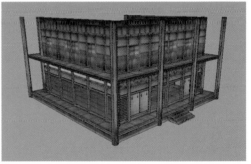

3. Create the walls.

Create the second floor. The smaller columns are drawn into the texture.

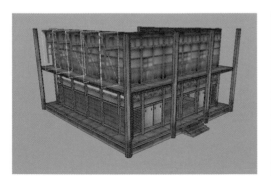

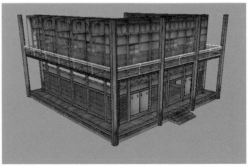

4. Create the beams with texture transparencies. Using flat polygons, the alpha channels can be 8-bit.

Please follow the project's game specifications when ordering the alpha priority of objects.

5. Create the handrails.

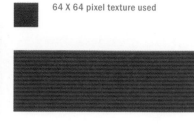

64 X 64 pixel texture used

6. Create the roof. The roof is not very visible to the camera. Use a smaller texture, but with a resolution that hides the stretching of the texture's width.

Completed model with textures

7. Place the minor items on the shirine, such as flags.

● **Production Process: Creating the Main Building**

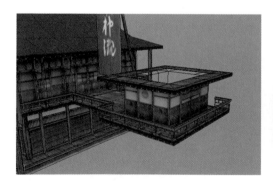

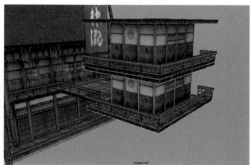

1. Start by creating the first floor.

2. Except for the handrails, instance copy the first floor to create the second.

Do not instance copy the handrails, which are slightly different in shape on the second floor.

3. Create the third floor and roof.

4. Place instance copies of the columns that are buried into the ground. Delete the polygons that are hidden from the camera.

5. Complete the main building by placing it on the ground.

Finished image

The color per vertex data

Excluding the polygons instance copied, the main shrine and building total 2,059 polygons

Finished image

Finished image

Chapter **11**

CREATING A RIVER

Introduction

A method called *UV animation* is generally used for animating textures, such as a river. UV animation creates movement within the UVs of seamless textures.

The UV animation setting controls the animation speed. In other words, the setting controls whether a game program animates the texture on one of the U and V axes, or both.

In terms of CG resources to animate, we only need to prepare a UV mapped model.

We will need to check the UV animation on-screen and adjust it.

As an alternate method, the game program can randomly animate UVs. The animation of water rippling is often created in this way.

Realism can be increased by using another method called *environmental mapping*, which artificially incorporates water reflection into a texture.

Here, the UVs are animated with a seamless texture with an alpha channel.

● New Term in this Chapter

UV animation: The method in which a game program animates the UVs of a UV-mapped model.

● UV Animation

Translating and animating the UV coordinates of an object is called UV scrolling. You can animate in the U direction V direction or both.

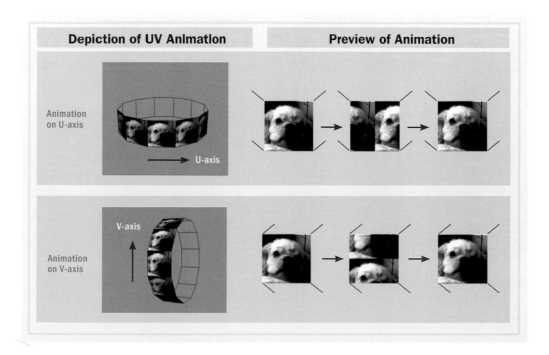

• UV Animation Textures

UV animate using a seamless texture.

When the texture has an alpha channel, ensure the alpha also becomes seamless.

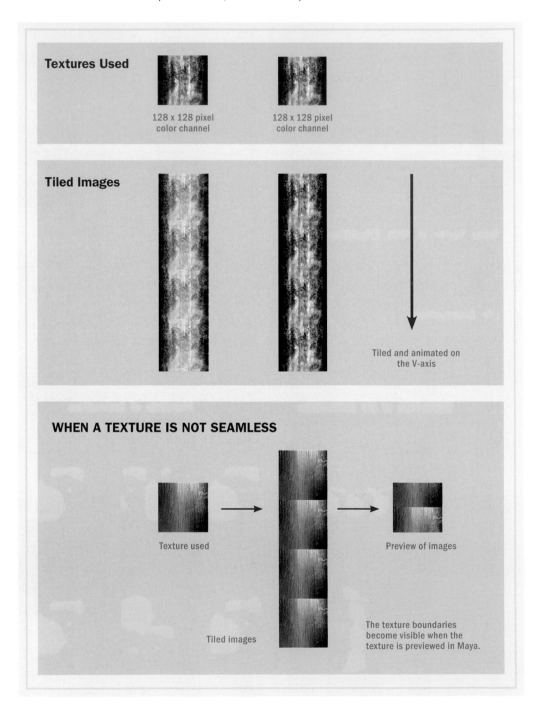

Textures Used

128 x 128 pixel
color channel

128 x 128 pixel
color channel

Tiled Images

Tiled and animated on
the V-axis

WHEN A TEXTURE IS NOT SEAMLESS

Texture used

Preview of images

Tiled images

The texture boundaries
become visible when the
texture is previewed in Maya.

Relationship of Polygon Size, UVs and UV Animation Speed

Person A runs 100 meters in 10 seconds, while Person B runs 50 meters in 10 seconds. In other words, Person A runs twice as fast as Person B.

The relative UV animation speed is the same. The game program's animation speed is identical for objects with identical properties.

In other words, when mapped by polygon units, the animation becomes faster as the polygons get larger.

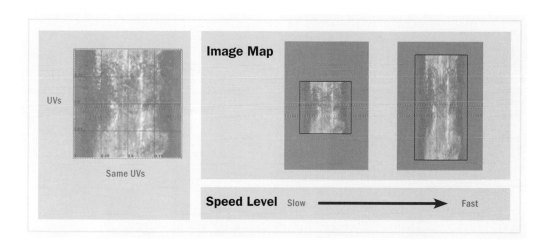

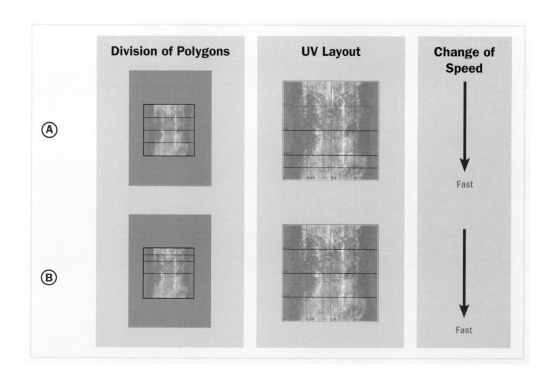

Furthermore, in diagram (A) on the previous page, the polygons are divided evenly in size before UV mapping. In such cases, the animation becomes faster with greater distance of the UVs.

In diagram (B), UV mapping is even. In such cases, the animations also become faster with greater polygon size.

In other words, diagrams (A) and (B) have the same animation speed. The UV animations are faster as they move down.

Animations can be shown that are effected by gravity, for example water accelerating as it falls towards the ground in a waterfall.

● **Production Process: Create a River**

Layout UVs.

128 x 128
pixel texture

Add vertex color.

The completed model
with textures.

Note: *A more realistic polygon model is improved by layering transparencies, i.e by applying 8-bit textures with alphas over top of each other. When doing so, we set the alpha priority .*

Chapter **12**
CREATE SKY & DISTANT BACKGROUND

Introduction

When creating the sky, consider how the clouds can be animated by also considering the camera's maximum angle in the game.

- ## New Term in this Chapter

  Multi-background Animation: The animation of the near background objects is faster, and that of the distant background objects is slower.

- ## Basic Distant Background

  In a game, a sky is commonly dome-shaped, allowing the camera to look up into it.

  When the camera cannot look up into it, the sky can be shaped into a cylinder or dome with the top part deleted.

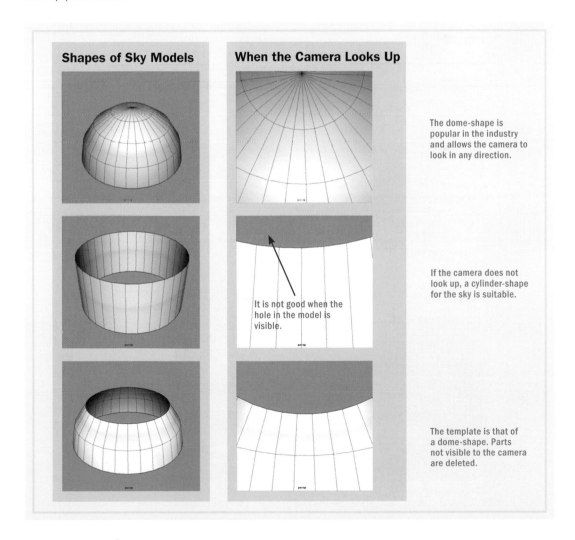

Shapes of Sky Models

When the Camera Looks Up

The dome-shape is popular in the industry and allows the camera to look in any direction.

It is not good when the hole in the model is visible.

If the camera does not look up, a cylinder-shape for the sky is suitable.

The template is that of a dome-shape. Parts not visible to the camera are deleted.

● Model Clouds, Mountains and Sky

Sky

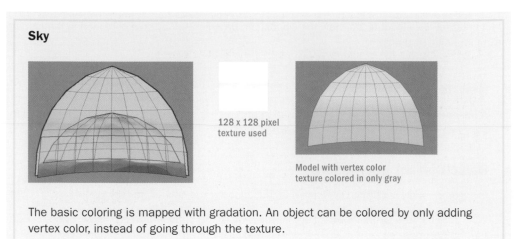

128 x 128 pixel
texture used

Model with vertex color
texture colored in only gray

The basic coloring is mapped with gradation. An object can be colored by only adding vertex color, instead of going through the texture.

Clouds

256 x 256 pixel
texture used

Non-transparencies
with vertex alphas

As well as the common dome-shaped sky, other backgrounds can be created, such as clouds and distant mountains.

Mountains

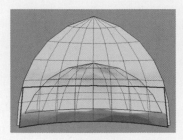

256 x 256 pixel textures
with 8-bit alphas used

The distant mountains are non-transparencies with alpha channels, and they blend with the sky backdrop.

- ## Animate Clouds

We have the option of either animating the actual cloud models or using UV animation to animate the clouds.

Furthermore, we can depict rolling clouds by manipulating the UVs within the game engine.

Rotating the Model Itself

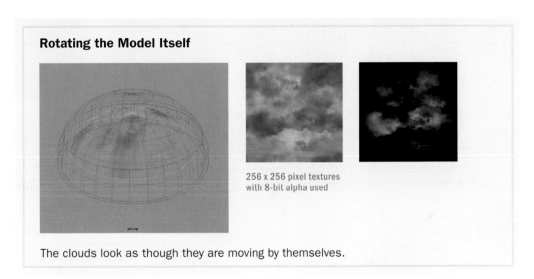

256 x 256 pixel textures with 8-bit alpha used

The clouds look as though they are moving by themselves.

UV Animation

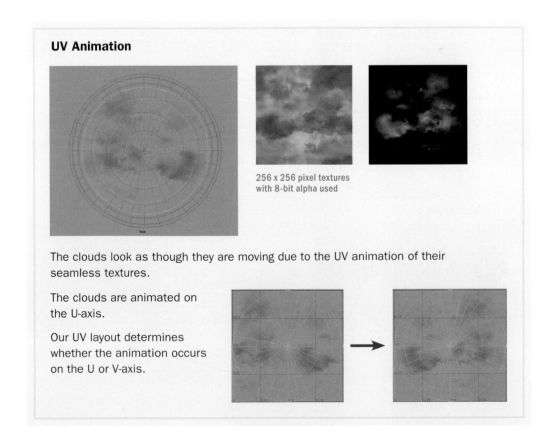

256 x 256 pixel textures with 8-bit alpha used

The clouds look as though they are moving due to the UV animation of their seamless textures.

The clouds are animated on the U-axis.

Our UV layout determines whether the animation occurs on the U or V-axis.

• Give Clouds Dimension

We can further accentuate the dimensions of the clouds by layering multiple cloud models.

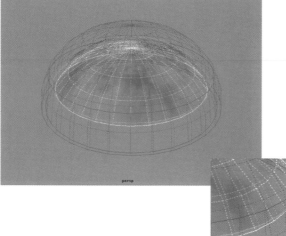

256 x 256 pixel textures
with 8-bit alphas used

The models are layered, and one layer is animated along the Y-axis (perpendicular to the ground).

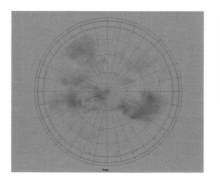 

Image of one model layer and its finished image

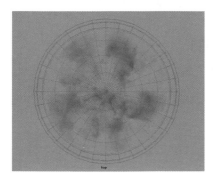 

Images of two model layers (with one layer rotated 90 degrees on the Y-axis), and its finished image

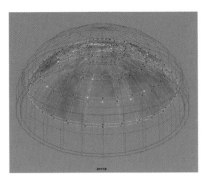 

The vertices of the vertex alphas are randomly selected, making the transparencies look more natural

Finished image

We should decide on factors (such as the number of cloud model layers) while checking the number of available polygons, if any, for the background map.

An alpha channel may not need to be added to the textures, instead use vertex alphas.

Check the clouds on-screen for the method that makes them look best.

• Path of the Sun and Vertex Color

We add vertex color to match the primary sky model to the sun's direction. When the game specifications require the cloud models to animate, we do not add the direction of the light to their vertex color. If we were to do so, the sun would also look like it animates, detracting from how the sky looks. We avoid the direction of the light on the clouds from being too obvious.

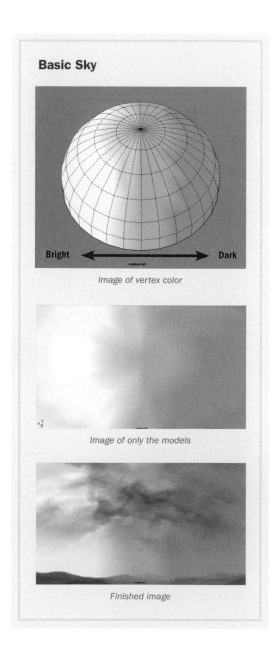

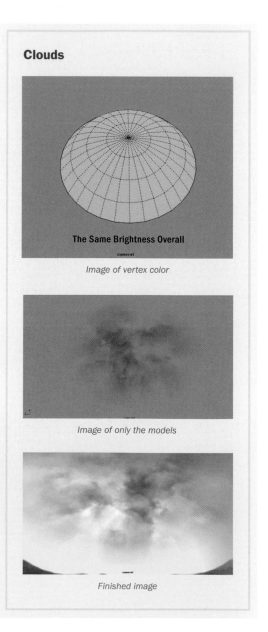

When the cloud models are animated, the brightness is the same for all clouds.

When UV animating, the light is illustrated into the vertex color.

The distant mountains closest to the sun are backlit the least. We add the bright vertex color to those mountains farthest from the sun.

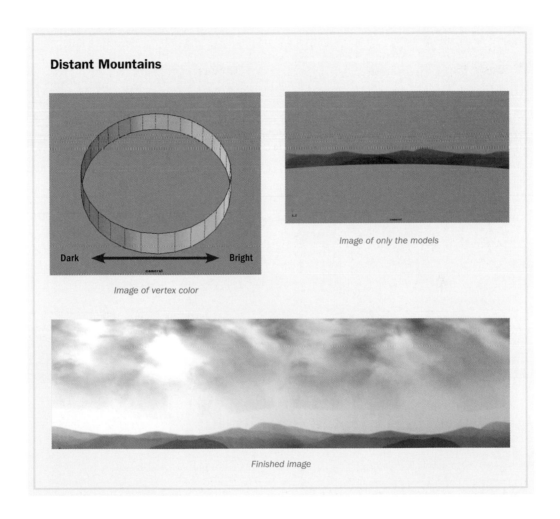

Distant Mountains

Dark ←——————→ Bright

Image of vertex color

Image of only the models

Finished image

● Mix Cloud, Mountain and Sky Animations

The common misconception is that clouds, mountains and sky are handled as a single background when displayed on-screen. However, the three can be animated separately, depending on the game engine.

In the real world, when we look off into the distance, things look as though they 'move' less with an increase in distance.

Without animating the sky background, we match the animation of the mountains with the camera movements. For the clouds, we animate the cloud models themselves or use UV animation.

In this way, when the near background scrolls relatively quickly, and the distant background scrolls relatively slowly, it is called multi-layer animation.

The mountain, sky with clouds and other background models all have to be separate for multi-layer animation. The reason being that a program handles all these models separately when converting them to display in a game.

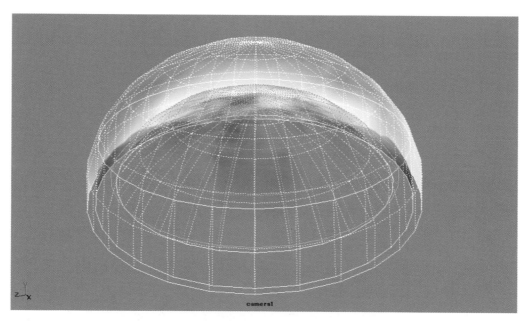

Models are all separate objects

Chapter 12

Without Multi-layer Animation

The distant mountains move with the camera.

With Multi-layer Animation

The distant mountains do not move very much despite the camera movement.

Be conscious of the composition between the house and mountains behind it.

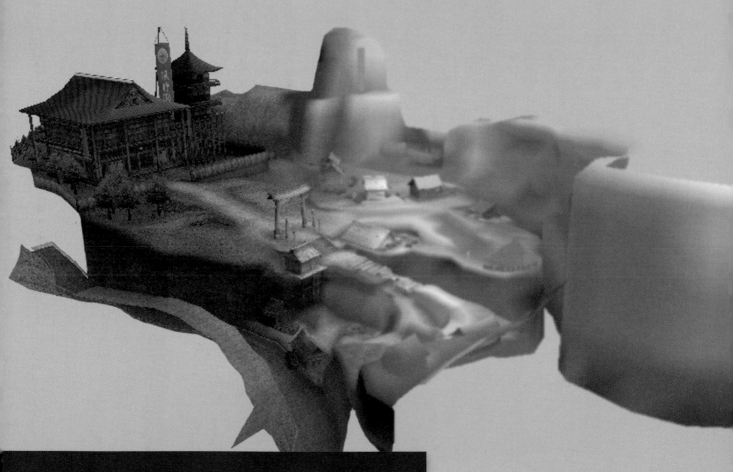

Chapter **13**

APPLYING VERTEX COLOR

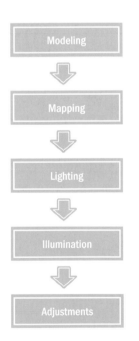

Introduction

Most games use a method that creates artificial lighting by setting the relevant color information in the polygon's vertex. This is called *vertex color.*

Currently, dynamic lighting can be set-up within a game, which is calculated for each object in real-time.

However, the use of vertex color is still the present norm within the industry.

With the model's textures unchanged, a single model can be used to show changes in the time of day (day, dusk, night). Only the object's colors and shadows need to be changed when setting up its vertex color.

● **New Terms in this Chapter**

Vertex Color Illumination: To add color and shadows that match the lighting to a vertex.

Pre-lighting: To apply lighting information from Maya to a vertex.

● **Pipeline to Vertex Color Application**

Modeling

⇩

Mapping

⇩

Lighting

⇩

Illumination

⇩

Adjustments

■ Color adjustment on a TV monitor
■ Polygon re-distribution
■ Remove edges

Vertex Color

The vertex color information is set-up as RGBA (Red, Green, Blue and Alpha).

Furthermore, the RGB settings are expressed between 0 to 255 or 0 and 1. The alpha is expressed between 0 and 1.

The RGBA setting of (128, 128, 128, 1) usually displays the default texture colors on-screen. The texture is completely black with an RGBA setting of (0, 0, 0, 1), and completely white with an RGBA setting of (255, 255, 255, 1).

However, the reality is that the texture colors displayed on-screen are often completely different. It is recommended to display the work on-screen periodically when making vertex color adjustments.

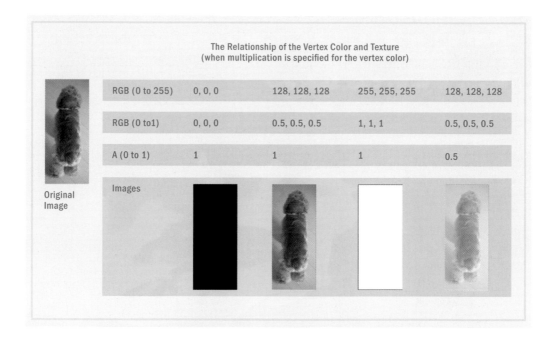

The Relationship of the Vertex Color and Texture
(when multiplication is specified for the vertex color)

	RGB (0 to 255)	0, 0, 0	128, 128, 128	255, 255, 255	128, 128, 128
	RGB (0 to1)	0, 0, 0	0.5, 0.5, 0.5	1, 1, 1	0.5, 0.5, 0.5
	A (0 to 1)	1	1	1	0.5
Original Image	Images				

> **Note:** *The programming of vertex color differs with every game production. Here multiplication is specified. However, the results on-screen differ completely if addition, etc. is used.*

Polygon Distribution and Vertex Color

Vertex color cannot be added to parts of an object without vertices.

To cast a shadow over a part without vertices, we must add detail to an object.

> **Note:** *How we apply vertex color changes with the direction polygons face after adding detail to them.*

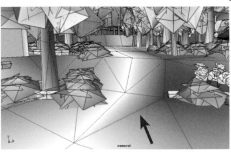
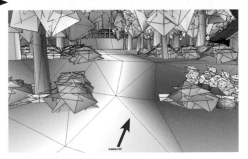

● Change the Time of the Day

As previously stated, the time of day can be changed for an object with how we apply vertex color.

According to the circumstances of the game production, we change our approach, such as changing the vertex color, to add detail to the polygons or to change the textures themselves.

Original Image

When the vertex color is fixed

When the texture is fixed

When polygons are added without changing the texture

● Smoothing Hard and Soft Edges

A model looks different depending on how the polygon edges are handled. The vertex color can be applied to the edges for them to look smooth (with a gradation), or to have distinct borders.

● Apply Vertex Color

1. Click on the vertex at the center. Although the polygon has only one vertex.

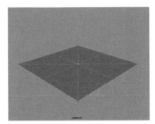

In vertex color mode, it is eight vertices assembled together.

We can make the vertex color settings on the various vertices by applying color to the vertex face.

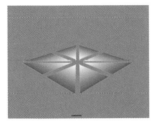

For example, if we set vertex color on all eight vertices, this is how it will look.

Note: *In Maya, a shared vertex can be detached and displayed separately.*

2. If we apply vertex color to four of the vertices.

This is how it will look.

3. If we apply vertex color to both ends of the four vertices.

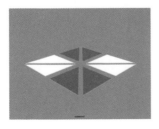

This checkered pattern results.

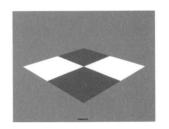

4. For a multi-sided object...

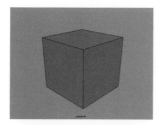

We apply vertex color to the individual object faces.

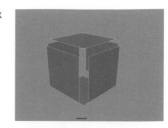

We apply vertex color to the top face and one at the side.

The dimension of the object stands out.

5. With the same multi-sided object...

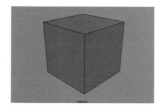

We apply vertex color to certain vertices.

The object has dimension, while its edges look smooth and have gradation.

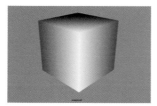

This way, a model's edges look different depending upon how the vertex color is applied. Using vertex color mode for hard edges, and the individual polygon vertices for soft edges help to differentiate them.

Now, we will look at how to specifically use each type of vertex color.

Vertex Color with Soft Edges   *Vertex Color with Hard Edges*

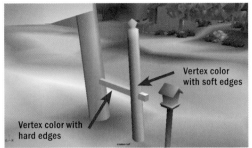

The vertex color is applied differently for pillars with soft and hard edges.

● Before Lighting

Types of Shadows

There are two types of shadows. One type is created behind the object on the ground when a light is aimed directly at an object. This is called a shadow. The other type is created when the light indirectly illuminates an object. This is called a shade.

Types of Lighting

Directional Light: Light that shines in the same direction with the same intensity, like sunlight.

It determines the color and intensity of the overall lighting, as well as the color of the shadows.

Ambient Light: In the real world, when not aimed directly at an object, reflected indirect light will still somewhat illuminate the object. This is called ambient light. In CG creation, the ambient light settings, such as the color of the shadows, can be changed.

Fundamentally, we should understand that an ambient light's intensity does not fade with greater distance from its epicenter, although this is not always the case.

Point Light: Like a small light bulb, a point light emits from one point.

Spotlight: Light that only shines on one location. It is shaped like a circle. The light fades in intensity with greater distance from its epicenter, compensating for any angles in the illuminated location.

● **Lighting: Pre-lighting**

Up until now, we have studied the fundamentals to lighting and applying vertex color.

In an actual game production, we first set-up lighting in Maya, add illumination and manually make the detailed adjustments.

Now, a basic explanation of lighting and vertex color illumination.

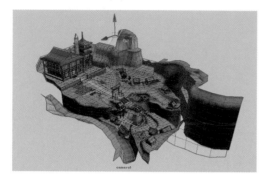

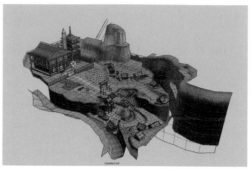

1. Create and position the directional light. Set the light's color, brightness and rate at which its brightness fades. Next, create and position the ambient light.

Positioning the ambient light opposite the directional light is recommended. Set the light's color, brightness and rate at which the brightness of the light fades.

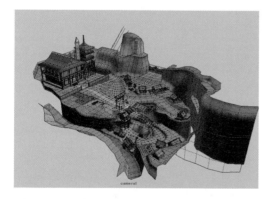

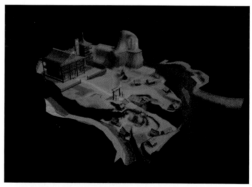

Lighting is adjusted while checking the rendered images, etc.

Position point lights and spotlights for locations we wish to highlight, or those that have their own light source, such as lamps.

Check the lighting through render images in Maya. After all the lighting settings are complete, proceed with illumination.

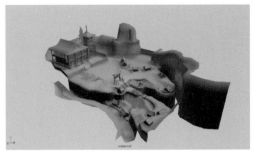

2. Add illumination for the vertex color.

Illuminate the vertex color in this way.

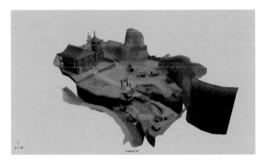

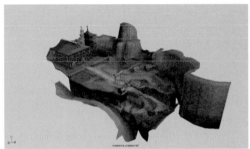

3. This is how the levels look when we apply textures. After checking how it looks on a TV monitor, adjust the brightness and color palette.

If it is too dark, then set-up the lighting and add illumination again.

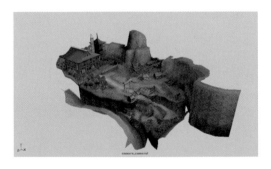

4. The adjustments are now complete.

5. The rest of the work is to be done manually. As explained in previously, add vertex color before laying out the trees.

Notes on Natural Things and Instance Copies

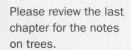

Please review the last chapter for the notes on trees.

As the instance copies will have the same vertex color as the original object, the direction of the light source (in the vertex color) should not be obvious.

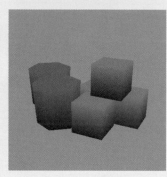

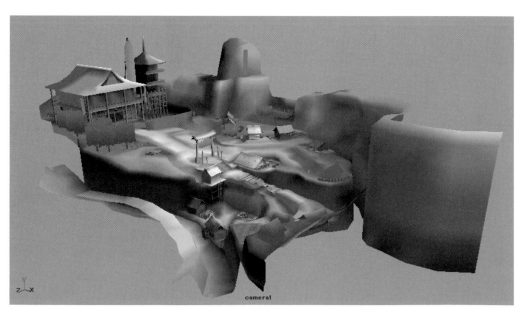

Vertex color

Finished image

> **Note:** *Adding the vertex color is manual work, but it makes setting up the lighting correctly all the more important. Each light is carefully set-up, as the lighting dramatically changes how the background looks.*

● Conclusion

In Section Three, we learned about the tools necessary to work on the game level.

More recent game productions also allow the manual setting of specular, environment and bump mapping.

The game production work environment has a multitude of tasks, and the current reality demands a flexible response to all of them.

After finishing modeling and UV mapping, the models are exported and read into the game engine.

The models are checked for bugs running within the game.

The additional settings are made in the game, such as fog, depth of field and anti-aliasing quality.

Other settings include collision and sound effects for a background environment, or for a character walking over a particular ground surface.

What remains are animation speed adjustments for any animated objects.

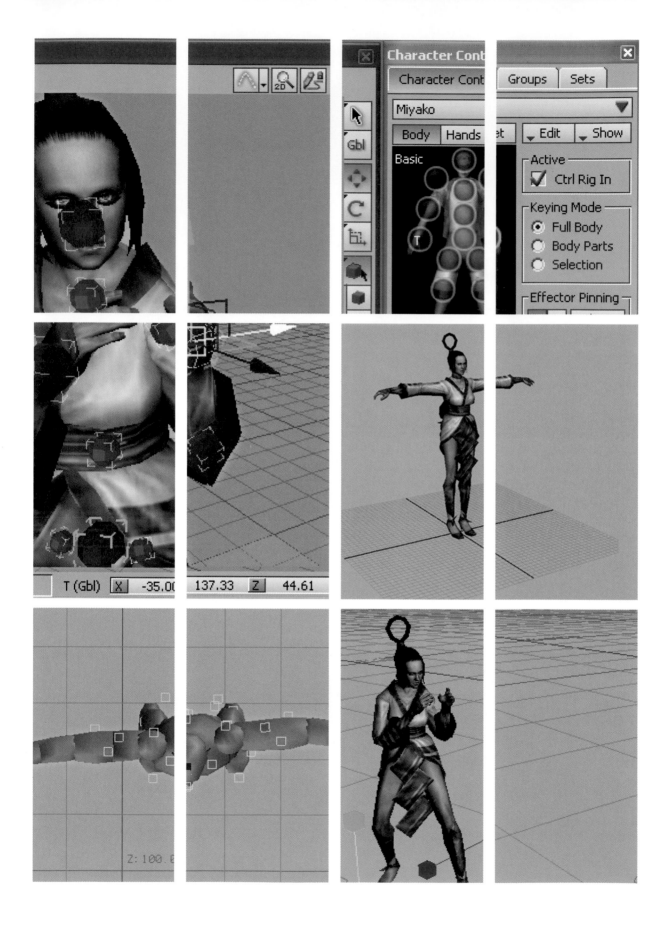

Section **Four**

ALIAS MOTIONBUILDER

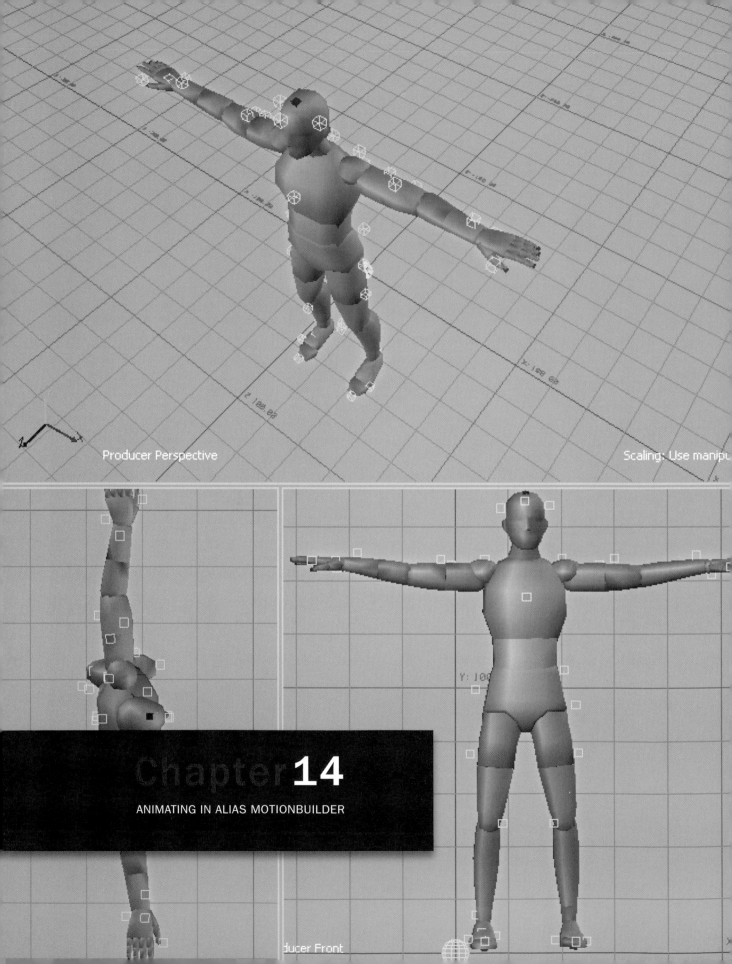

Scaling: Use manipu

Chapter **14**

ANIMATING IN ALIAS MOTIONBUILDER

Introduction

In this chapter, we will learn how to use Alias MotionBuilder to animate the Miyako character. Alias MotionBuilder is a specialized animation tool designed to quickly generate high quality character performances and animation. It's based on unique real-time architecture, intelligent character animation technology (HumanIK®) and motion capture performance tools.

This chapter is designed to help you achieve the following goals:

- Give you the tools to quickly create character animation and edit it;

- Introduce you to the Alias MotionBuilder UI and its main tools;

- Acquire an understanding of a Maya and Alias MotionBuilder pipeline;

- Establish a consistent standard character preparation workflow;

- Facilitate the use of motion capture data;

- Provide knowledge of the animation editing tools.

● Why use Alias MotionBuilder?

Alias MotionBuilder is specifically designed for character animation.

Its advantages include:

- Fast and easy creation of powerful character rigs, including facial setups;

- Real-time playback;

- Support of almost all existing types of motion capture data and devices;

- Intuitive tools designed for keyframing animations and editing with motion capture data;

- Most advanced tools for character animation retargeting;

- A smooth learning curve, since it also relies on standard animation controls and other 3D packages.

The Alias MotionBuilder Workflow

Although Alias MotionBuilder has some basic modeling and texturing tools, it relies on other 3D packages like Maya for character modeling and texturing. The transition between Alias MotionBuilder and other packages is done with the FBX® file format, which we will look at in the next section.

A standard pipeline for games using Alias MotionBuilder would follow this workflow:

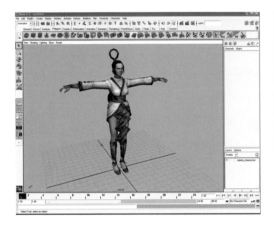

1. In Maya, the character is modeled using NURBS or polygons. Its geometry is then binded to a skeleton and textured. The character is exported in the FBX format and sent to Alias MotionBuilder. No rigs or setups are required for the character from Maya.

2. In Alias MotionBuilder, the character is rigged and animated in real-time using motion capture, traditional keyframes and other tools specific to character animation. The file is saved once more in the FBX format.

3. The new FBX file is merged back in the original Maya file, transferring the animations.

• Working with FBX

FBX is the native file format from Alias MotionBuilder. It has become a standard format for interchanging data between 3D packages.

The FBX file format has been integrated into Maya since version 6.5. The FBX plug-ins for previous Maya versions are available on the Alias web site (www.alias.com).

This file format supports the following features:

- Polygons
- NURBS
- UV textures
- Skeleton
- Smooth bind weight maps

- Blend shapes
- Cluster deformers
- Lights
- Cameras
- Animations

> **Note:** *Keep in mind that construction history is not supported and there are some limitations regarding the options of these features. Please refer to the FBX plug-in documentation for a full description.*

Exporting Miyako

At this point, we need to export Miyako from Maya in the FBX format using the **Export All** command (**File** → **Export All**).

Next, go to the **Export All** options and choose **FBX** as the file type. We also need to maintain the default options for the **FBX Exporter**.

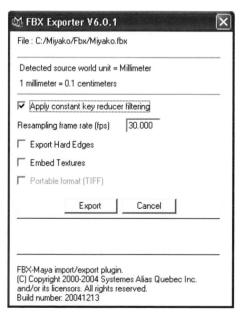

The FBX Exporter option window

Navigating in Alias MotionBuilder – Hotkeys

The basic Maya hotkeys are supported in Alias MotionBuilder. You can activate them in the **Settings** menu by choosing **Settings → keyboard configuration → Maya**.

Here's a quick list of the supported hotkeys:

Maya Hotkeys Supported in Alias MotionBuilder

Alt+LMB, Alt+MMB and Alt+RMB	Camera controls; tumble, track and dolly
f	Frame selection
4, 5, 6 and 7	Display type; wireframe, shaded, textured
z and Ctrl+z	Undo and redo
s	Set key
Ctrl+n, Ctrl+o and Ctrl+s	File new, open and save
Up, down, right and left key arrows	Navigating in a hierarchy

> **Note:** *Any **drag+drop** is done with the **X+LMB** combo using Maya hotkeys.*
>
>
>
> ** This chapter uses the Maya hotkey configurations.*

Preparing Miyako for Animation

Right after starting Alias MotionBuilder, we will set the UI layout to editing (**Layout → Editing**) to avoid any UI discrepancies with this book.

In the next steps, we will prepare Miyako to begin animation.

Loading up Miyako

There are two ways of loading or merging a file in Alias MotionBuilder.

In the **File** menu, choose **Open** (**Ctrl+o**) and **Merge** commands for loading of merging files in the current scene.

The second option is the **Asset Browser**. This window located in the lower right corner is helpful for quickly browsing, loading and previewing frequently used files.

The Asset Browser UI is divided into two sections. By default, the folders are located on the left section (**A**) and the files on the right (**B**). Note that only the supported file formats will appear in this section. There are also some display options in the upper part of the Asset Browser. They are used to control the general display of the Asset Browser (**C**) and the file display (**D**).

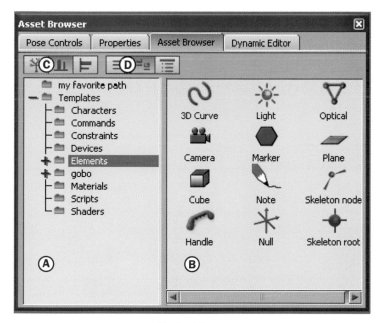

The Asset Browser

One of the main advantages of the Asset Browser is the ability to preview the contents of the file without opening it. This is available in the **Thumbnails** or **List** file display mode (in the D section).

The Asset Browser also contains a *Templates* folder that includes all the assets that can be created in Alias MotionBuilder, such as constraints, materials, lights, cameras and some primitives.

For loading or creating assets, you simply need to **drag+drop** the asset in the 3D viewer (camera's view) using the **LMB**.

To add the project in the Asset Browser, **RMB+click** anywhere in the folder area (**A**) and select the option **Add favorite path**, and then select the folder containing the Miyako FBX file. Finally, drag the Miyako FBX file anywhere in the 3D viewer.

Adjusting Miyako

Before we start to animate Miyako, we will make a few adjustments in order to have a cleaner visual feedback of the character.

Scaling Miyako

Alias MotionBuilder preserves the world scale of Maya, which is in centimeters by default. Often the characters are only a few centimeters high in Maya, and we need to scale them up in Alias MotionBuilder for easier selection and visualization. This step is optional, but highly recommended.

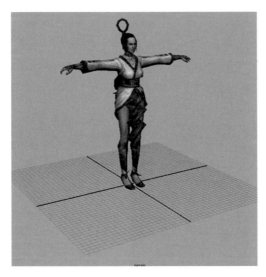

Maya grid, 1 square = 1cm. The character is about 18 cm high

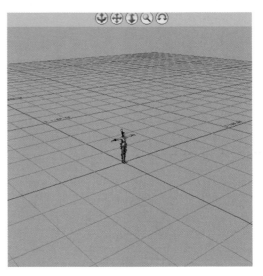

Alias MotionBuilder grid, 1 square = 20cm. The character remains the same size, about 18 cm high.

To scale up Miyako, we will select her master node in the Alias MotionBuilder scene browser, the **Navigator**.

The Navigator is quite similar to the Maya **Outliner**. It lists all the assets of your scene **(A)**, and the **Asset Settings (B)** area displays the settings of the selected asset.

We will now open the Scene node and select the Reference node.

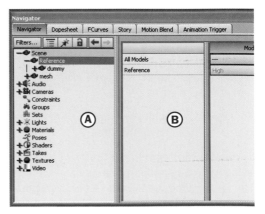

The Reference node in the Navigator

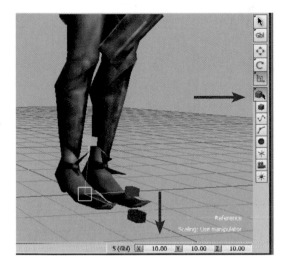

Once the Reference node is selected, scale it up by 10.

To scale it, you can drag the scaling manipulator (E key), or enter precise scaling values in the lower corner of the 3D viewer. In this case, we need to put 10, 10 and 10 for the X, Y and Z values.

Changing the Joints' Size

We will also need to adjust the joints' size. Toggle through the different display types to switch to the X-ray display using the **Ctrl+a** keys. This will make the joints fully visible.

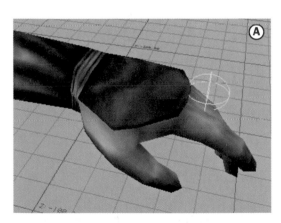

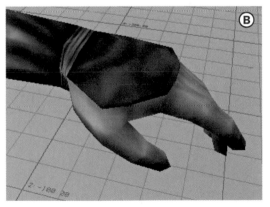

To select all the joints, **LMB-click** and create a marquee selection around the entire skeleton in the 3D viewer. We don't need to worry about all the other elements, like locators, that might have been selected at the same time.

Display Type: **A:** Normal, **B:** Models only, **C:** X-ray

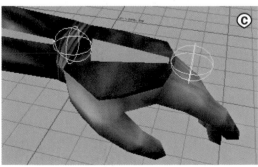

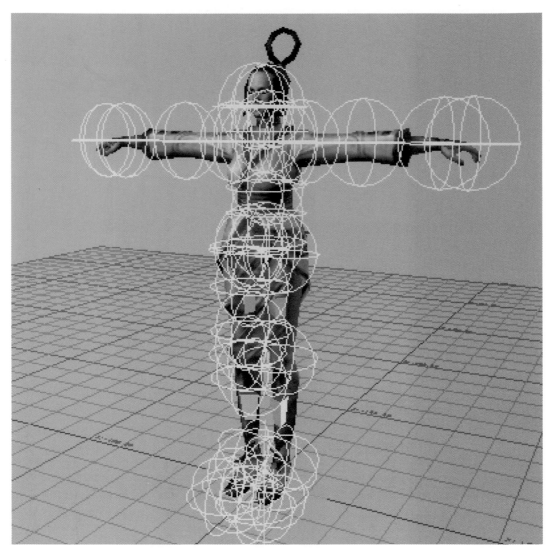

Miyako's oversized joints

To change all the joint sizes simultaneously, use the **Properties Editor**.

The properties are the equivalent of Maya attributes, and they are accessible in the **Properties Editor**, in the lower-right corner.

By default, the objects are grouped by type in the **Properties Editor**. This makes editing a common property quite easy.

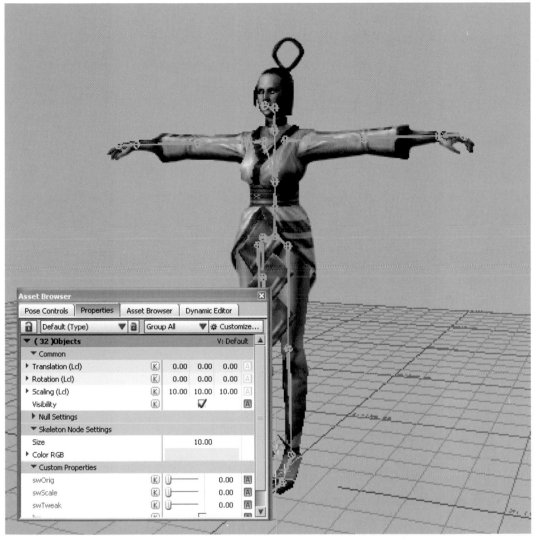

Fixed joints' size

In this case, the size of the joints would be the common property to edit. Go to the **Skeleton Node Settings** and change the size from 100 to 10 for a proper joint size.

By selecting the **No grouping option** instead of the default **Group All**, the Properties Editor will list the properties of each object individually, like the Maya Attribute Editor.

This will allow for example joints with different sizes and colors for better visual feedback.

• Characterization of Miyako

Characterization Concept

Characterization is a process unique to Alias MotionBuilder. It identifies or labels the joints of a character in order to animate and manipulate them correctly. This process is necessary for any characters brought into Alias MotionBuilder and should be one of the first steps right after importing a character. If the joints are named properly, the characterization becomes almost an automatic process.

Once the characterization is done, it allows us to apply Motion Capture data to a character. This is also called Actor Input.

Actor input, or optical motion capture data input

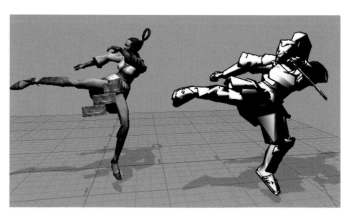

It also allows us to retarget pre-existing animations from one character to another one. This is called the Character Input, and it can only be done when the two characters are characterized.

Character input

Finally, characterization allows us to create a control rig, which is a manipulation rig for keyframed animations. This rig is used to either create animation from scratch or to edit existing animations.

Control Rig input

> **Note**: *Before characterizing, we need to ensure the character is facing the positive Z-axis. It should also be in a T-stance, like the Miyako binding position.*

• Characterization Process

To characterize Miyako, we need to go in the **Asset Browser**, drag the **Character** template (**Asset Browser** → **Character**) onto any Miyako joint and click on the Characterize pop-up. If Miyako's joints are not visible, use the **Ctrl+a** keys until you see the skeleton. Ctrl+a toggles between different display types: **Normal**, **Models** only and **X-ray**.

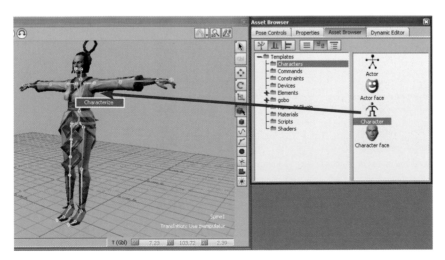

The Characterization process

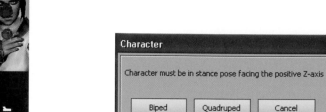

Character types

After clicking on the Characterize pop-up, we need to choose a biped characterization since Miyako is a two-legged character.

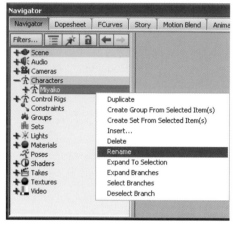

Renaming the character Miyako

Once Miyako has been characterized, a Character folder will appear in the Navigator. Open this folder and rename the character Miyako by **RMB+clicking** on it.

Modifying a Characterization

By **double-clicking** on Miyako in the **Navigator**, this opens up the settings of this character.

Under the **Character Definition** tab, we can see Miyako joint associations to the character template (**A**). This process is based on the joint names matching up identical names. In our case, Miyako joint names in the Model list (**B**) follow the template names (**A**), allowing an automatic characterization.

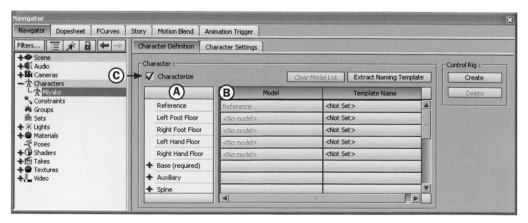

Character definition

To unlock, modify or create associations, we need to uncheck the **Characterize checkbox (C)**, and then **LMB+x** drag any joints from the viewer in the proper space in the Model list **(B)**.

> **Note:** *This checkbox should always be unchecked while the character is in its characterization pose or T-stance, otherwise that original stance position will be lost.*

In our case, the characterization of the joints doesn't have to be changed, but in the next section, we will need to add the left and right foot references in the Model list to create an automatic floor contact detection.

Setting up Miyako's Floor Contact

Floor Contact is a setup that prevents the feet/hands from going through a defined floor, and it also takes care of the toes'/fingers' animations while the feet/hands are interacting with the floor.

Defining the Floor Level

We will use a standard plane as a reference for the floor level. To create a plane, go to **Asset Browser** → **Templates** → **Elements**, and **drag+drop** a plane in the 3D viewer. We will translate this plane at position 0 on the Y-axis.

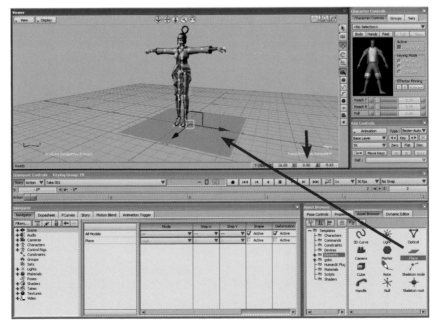

Plane creation from the Asset Browser

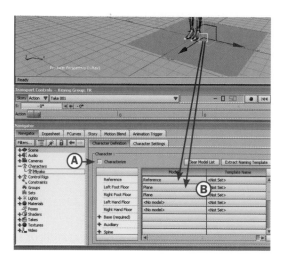

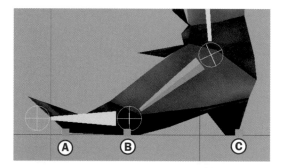

Using the plane as the floor level for the feet

We will now associate this plane to the Miyako characterization. In order to do that, we need to gain access to the Model list (**Characters** → **Miyako** → **Character Definition** tab) of our character by unchecking the Characterize checkbox (A).

Once this is done, we will **drag+drop** (**LMB+x+drag**) the plane in the **Left** and **Right Foot Floor** sections into the Model List (**B**) of the Character Definition. After the plane has been dropped in the two foot floor sections, we will check the **Characterize box** once more (**A**) to lock these changes and confirm the characterization.

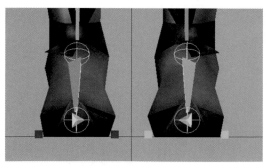

Foot markers A: Heel contact B: Toes bending C: Toes contact

Adjusting the foot floor markers

The floor markers define the contact area (**A,C**) and the bending section (**B**) of the feet. Starting from the back (**A**), we will adjust the markers as shown to the left view (**Ctrl+r**) and the front view (**Ctrl+f**). Once this is done, **Ctrl+e** will bring us back to the Perspective camera.

Note: *If the floor markers are not visible, switch to **X-ray** or **Normal display (Ctrl+a)**. These markers can also be hidden using the show menu in the **Character Controls** window.*

Show floor contact

Finally, activate the **Feet Floor Contact** in the **Character Settings** tab under the Floor **Contacts** section (**Character → Character Settings → Floor Contacts → Feet Floor Contact**).

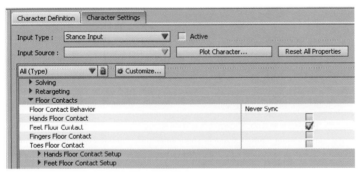

Floor Contact activation in the Character Settings

We will see later in the animation section how the **Floor Contact** helps the animation of a character's feet.

The character preparation for Miyako is now done and she's ready to be animated.

Foot rotation with no floor contact (A), with floor contact activated (B)

● **Animating Miyako**

We will now animate Miyako using Motion Capture data and some keyframe animations.

Loading up Motion Capture Animations

We will append some Motion Capture animation to the current file. Under the **File** menu, we will import a file named *punch.c3d* (**File** → **Import**). C3d is a common Motion Capture file format for optical data, which we will discuss later in this section. The default options should be used in the **Import** window.

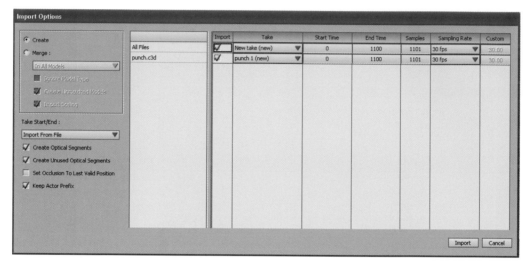

Import options for the c3d file

Once the file has been imported, we should see light blue markers in the 3D viewer representing a human form. Press the play button to see the animations of these markers. If no markers are visible, press **Ctrl+a** to toggle between the different display types.

You can also view these markers in the Schematic View (**Ctrl+w** or **Viewer** → **View** → **Schematic**).

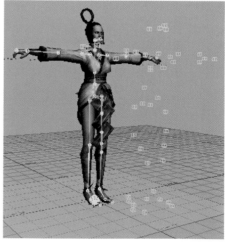

C3d markers

The Schematic View is similar to the Hypergraph in Maya; it shows the nodes of the scene with all the hierarchies. If the view is not well organized, we can **RMB+click** in the window and choose the **Arrange All** command.

In Alias MotionBuilder, all the Motion Capture data has a similar hierarchy as this c3d one. It has a parent node (**C3D:optical**) and all the markers are to be located directly beneath it. The parent node is also represented as a sphere in the 3D viewer (**Ctrl+e**). It can be used to reposition the animation in 3D space when translated.

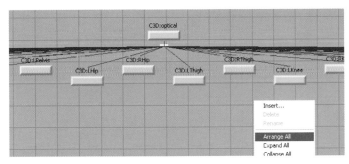
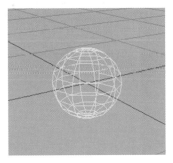

Schematic View   *C3d Parent node in the 3D viewer*

Optical Motion Capture data animations usually consist of translation animation curves. This is due to the nature of the Motion Capture system itself; its cameras 'see' points moving in space.

Since skeleton animation is essentially based on rotational information (put aside the squash and stretch effects), we will need to convert these translation animations into rotation animations.

We will see how this can be easily done using an actor.

Applying Motion Capture

The Actor

The animations of these markers are transferred to a character via an actor. The actor basically takes the translation animation of the markers and transfers them to its body parts as rotation animation.

Before we create an actor, we will hide Miyako to have a cleaner view. **Ctrl+Shift+RMB** on one of her joints and then **Ctrl+Shift+RMB** again on any part of her geometry. This command has selected the entire hierarchy of the joints and geometry. Press **Shift+h** to hide her (**Ctrl+h** again to display her).

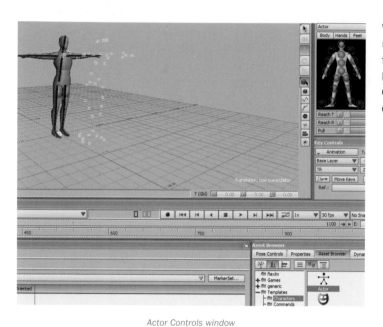

We will now create an actor using the Asset Browser templates folder (**Asset Browser** → **Templates** → **Character** → **Actor**), with the **drag+drop** as shown to the left.

Actor Controls window

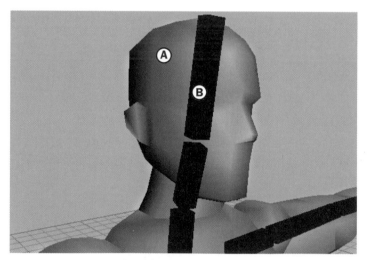

Actor's body parts and skeleton

For now, we will hide the skeleton using the Actor Controls, Show menu in the upper-right corner.

As we did with the character, we will rename this actor in Navigator by **RMB+clicking** on its name. We will name him *ActionMan*.

Visually, the actor consists of body parts (**A**) in light gray and a skeleton (**B**) in dark gray.

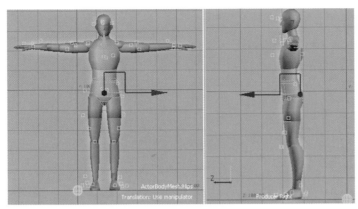

At frame zero when the markers form a T-stance, we will select the hips and translate and rotate them so the actor matches the markers.

Actor body parts position

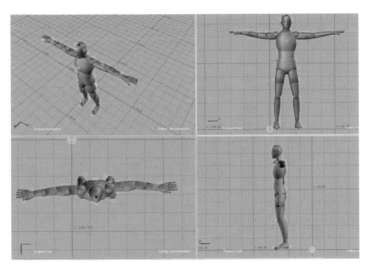

The body parts need to be translated, scaled and rotated so they also match the markers as shown to the left.

We will now associate the markers to the proper actor body parts, using a MarkerSet.

To create a MarkerSet, open the *Actors* folder in the Navigator (Outliner) and **double-click** on the *ActionMan*. This brings up the **Actor Settings**. On the right side of the Actor Settings, click on the **MarkerSet** button and choose **Create**.

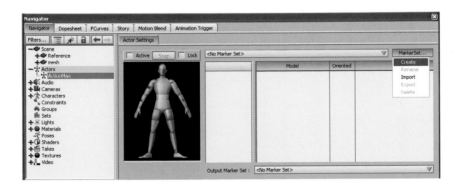

We will now associate these markers with the actor body parts by **drag+dropping (LMB+x)** them in the Actor Settings (**A**), at frame zero when the markers form a T-stance.

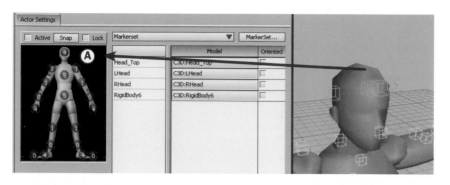

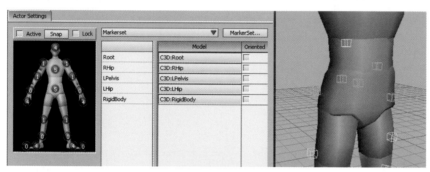

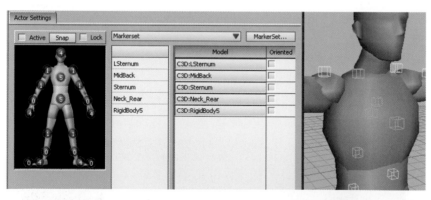

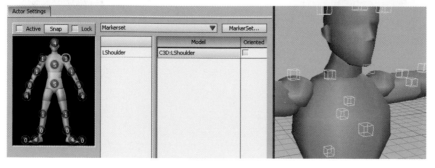

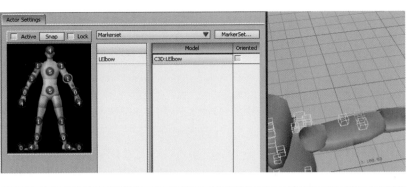

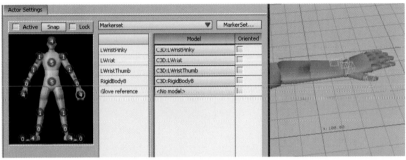

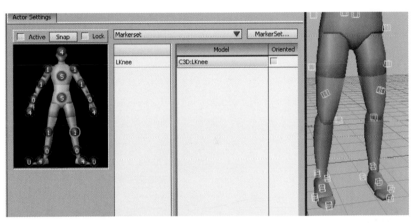

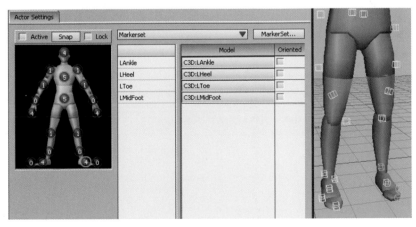

Repeat these steps for the body parts on the left side.

To activate the link between the markers and the actor, check the Active checkbox (A). Once this is done, the actor will follow the markers. The markers' translation animation curves have been converted into body part rotations.

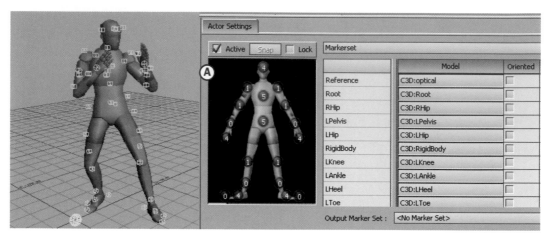

Active checkbox (A)

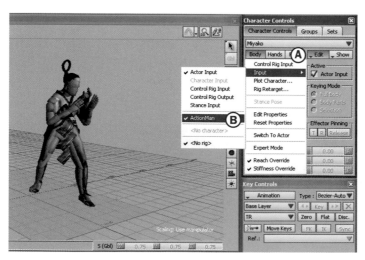

Actor input activation

We can now use this actor as a source of animation for Miyako. Unhide her by pressing **Ctrl+h** while nothing is selected.

In the **Character Controls** window (A), go in the **Edit** menu and choose the actor ActionMan input (B).

When we activate this input, Miyako will immediately follow the actor motion.

To create an offset between the actor and Miyako for better viewing purposes, we will select the Reference node (A), located between Miyako's feet in the Character Controls window, and we will translate it along the X-axis.

The actor can be hidden using the **Character Controls → Show (B)** if desired.

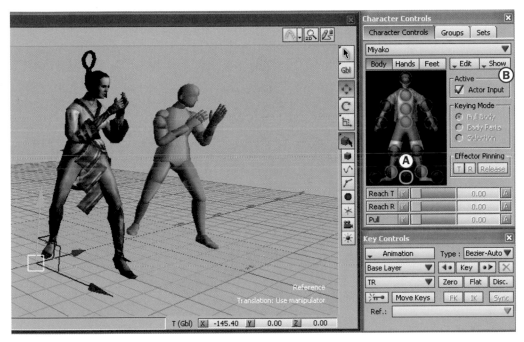

Character Controls window

● **Editing Motion Capture Animation**

When using an actor input, the character animations sometimes need adjustments. This is due to the different physiognomy between the actor and the character.

For instance, at the 377th frame, we can clearly see some problems with the Miyako animation. Her hands are going through each other while the actor looks fine. This is caused by the length of Miyako's limbs, which are not quite similar to the actor's. To fix that, we will use a control rig.

Hands problem with actor input

• The Control Rig

The control rig is a powerfull forward kinematic (FK) and inverse kinematic (IK) setup to animate and edit character animations . It's a full body rig unique to Alias MotionBuilder and as we will see, it is created easily and quickly.

To create a control rig for Miyako, we will go in the **Character Controls** window and select **Plot Character...** from the **Edit** menu.

We will need to choose the Control Rig (A) and FK/IK (B) options in the pop-ups shown to the right. Finally, leave the plotting options as they are and click on Plot (C).

This basically creates a full forward kinematic (FK) and inverse kinematic (IK) body rig onto Miyako without affecting the current animation.

The control rig on Miyako is represented by yellow markers (FK) and blue/red markers (IK).

These markers received a copy of the Motion Capture animation curves during the plotting process. We can view these animation curves by selecting a marker and its rotation properties in the Fcurves window.

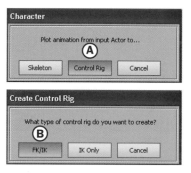

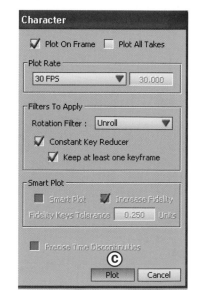

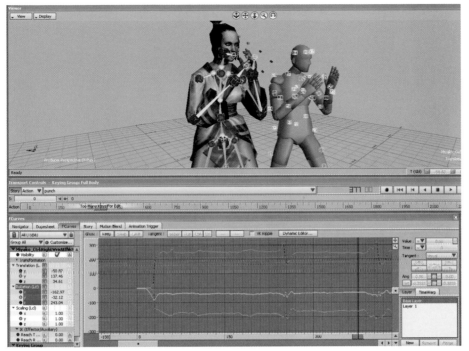

Fcurves window

Fcurves Window

The Fcurves window is the equivalent of the Maya Graph Editor.

It lets you create, view and modify function curves (animation curves) in various ways. For example, you can control the interpolation between keyframes, a curve's extrapolation and the value and time of the function curve.

By selecting a marker and its rotation properties in the Fcurves window, we can see that these curves have one keyframe per frame and this makes them very hard to edit properly. We will see in the next section how we can use layers to easily edit Motion Capture animation.

Animation Layers

To avoid dealing with numerous keyframes, we will create an animation layer free of keyframes.

The animation layers are created in the **Key Controls** window, under the **Base Layer** pull-down menu. Select the one layer that's already created by default, **Layer 1**.

Creation of Layer1

We will now switch to **X-ray display** mode (**Ctrl+a**) and keyframe the IK handles of the hands. To better view the IK handles, we will hide the skeleton and the FK using the **Character Controls → Show** menu and unchecking the **Skeleton** and **FK** options.

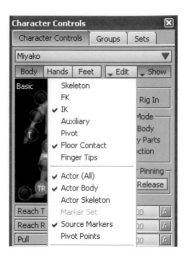

Now, we can increase the distance between the hands by selecting the hands' IK handles from the viewer (**A**), or in the Character Controls window (**B**) and spreading them apart. Once this is done, we will press the **Key** button (**C**) in the **Key Control** window to keyframe this offset.

Hiding the FK system and skeleton

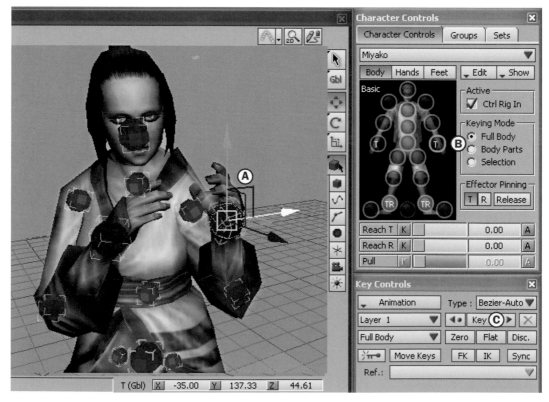

Keyframing an offset on the hands' IK handles

• Bringing Miyako Animation Back into Maya

Plotting the Animation onto Miyako's Joints

In order to bring this animation back into Maya, we will now transfer it onto Miyako's original Maya joints by again using **Plot Character...** from the **Edit** menu, but this time we will also use both the **Skeleton** button (**A**) in the pop-up and the default plotting option. The plotting process flattens the layers, collapsing all the animation onto the base layer for the selected character.

Plot character

Scaling Back Miyako

Now that Miyako is animated, we will scale back to her original size to bring her back into Maya. We need to select the Reference node and scale it back from 10 to 1 on the X, Y and Z-axis.

Plot on skeleton

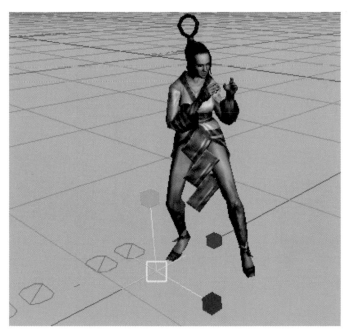

Scaling back Miyako at 1, 1, 1 using the Reference node

Saving Miyako as an FBX File

We will now save the scene and import it back into Maya. We will use the **File** → **Save as** command and name the new file *Miyako2.fbx* with the default options as shown in the image to the right.

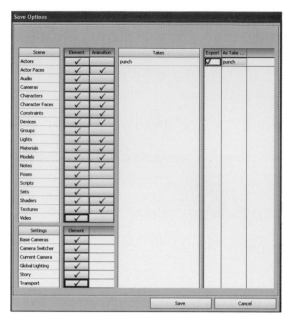

Save options window

Importing the File into Maya

In Maya, we need to load the original Miyako Maya scene and then import (**File** → **Import**) the *Miyako2.fbx* file using the **Exclusive Merge** option (A) and selecting the punch take (B). This will merge only already existing elements in Maya and will only transfer the punch animation.

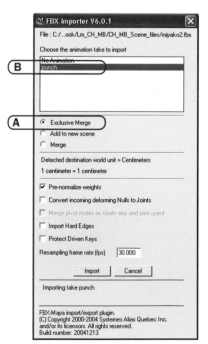

FBX importer options

FBX importer warning for locked attributes

> **Note:** *When attributes are locked in Maya, it prevents the FBX importer from transferring the animation. Hence, a warning window will pop-up, asking if these attributes should be unlocked or not.*

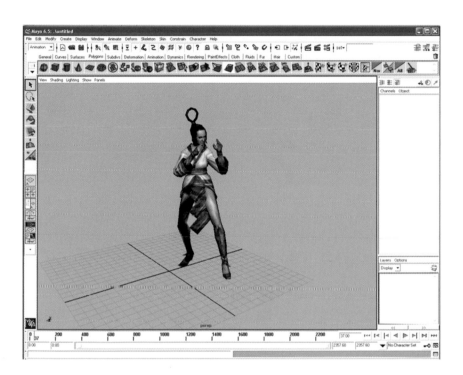

Result in Maya

The animation is now transferred in Maya.

● Conclusion

This chapter afforded you a glimpse into the power of Alias MotionBuilder. Its character oriented tools and real-time display capability greatly speed up games' pipelines where too often, the character animation is the bottleneck.

We have touched upon the basics of some of the main tools of Alias MotionBuilder. We have seen how to quickly animate a character from Maya in Alias MotionBuilder by using Motion Capture and keyframe editing. This chapter also included a preparation phase consisting of scaling up the character and setting up its characterization and floor contact. Finally, we saw how to bring back animations from Alias MotionBuilder into Maya.

Alpha channel: The data that stores information of a texture's transparency level. The data is stored as an 8-bit grayscale or a 1-bit black-and-white texture.

Alpha priority: A priority order that needs to be given to the polygons with 8-bit alpha channel textures. The order is relative to a polygon's distance from the camera compared to the other polygons. In giving an alpha priority, the transparent parts are easily removed.

Collision: The term is also known as the contact setting. It determines when a character, wall, etc. makes contact.

Depth of field: A setting to determine the distances to blur distant backgrounds. With a low depth of field setting, objects are blurred from locations near the camera.

Dual-sided polygon: A polygon that displays the textures both in the direction of the face normal and in the opposite direction.

Instance object: An object created when instance copy is used on another object. This instance object is like a facsimile. Even if several instance copies are placed on-screen, as long as they are copied from the same object, they reduce the total file size. For example, a forest is often created from the instance objects of one tree object.

MIP map: A CG function to use a high-resolution texture for an object near the camera, and a low-resolution texture for a distant object (and the object appears smaller on-screen).

Multi-background animation: The animation of the faster near backgrounds and slower distant backgrounds.

Normal: An indicator of which way a polygon is facing. It uses a vector vertical to the plane of the polygon.

One-sided polygon: A polygon that only displays a texture in the direction of the face normal.

Pre-lighting: Adding lighting information on a vertex with CG tools.

Seamless texture: A tileable texture drawn so all its borders are not visible when applied.

Sound effects: Effects to develop the audio mood of a game.

Tessellation: A CG function that divides polygons into triangles to render a model on-screen.

Texture sheet: Like a jigsaw puzzle, a sheet combining numerous smaller textures together. The sheet still needs to be within the game production's texture size restrictions.

Tiling: A method that sets the number of times to repeatedly apply a texture, analogous to conventional tiling inside a house.

UV animation: A game program method for animating the UVs of a UV-mapped model.

UV mapping: A method for mapping onto an object using a texture's UV coordinates (instead of the XYZ space coordinates). By adjusting the top-most vertices of a polygon mesh on the UV-axis, we can easily apply a smaller texture to a texture sheet.

Vertex alpha: A method that stores alpha information in top-most vertices of a polygon, instead of a texture's alpha channel.

Vertex color illumination: Adding color to the vertex.

Z Sort algorithm: An algorithm that orders the polygons and first displays the ones with their centers farthest from the camera on-screen.

Z Buffer algorithm: An algorithm that orders and displays polygons on-screen by their pixel units.

Maya™ 7

changing the face of 3D

Alias®

Silver Membership

GET MORE OUT OF MAYA®
with the Maya Silver Membership program!

As award-winning software, Maya® is the most comprehensive 3D and 2D graphics and animation solution on the market. And whether you're using Maya Personal Learning edition to learn more about computer graphics and animation, or you have a full Maya license that you're using to produce professional content, the Maya Silver Membership program helps you take your Maya skill to the next level.

What is Maya Silver Membership?

Your Maya Silver Membership program gives you quick, online access to a wide range of Maya learning resources. These educational tools – in-depth tutorials; real-life, project-based learning materials; the Maya Mentor learning environment plug-in; Weblogs from experienced Maya users – are available for a fixed monthly, or cost-saving annual, subscription fee.

Silver Membership also keeps you abreast of the latest computer graphics industry developments and puts you in touch with other Maya users and industry experts. Plus, you get 30 days of personal help to orient you around the site.

Key Benefits

- **Unbeatable Value**
- **Faster Learning**
- **Competitive Advantage**
- **Industry Contacts**

For more information visit www.alias.com/silver

watching your every move ...

red eye studio

1.847.843.2438
www.redeye-studio.com

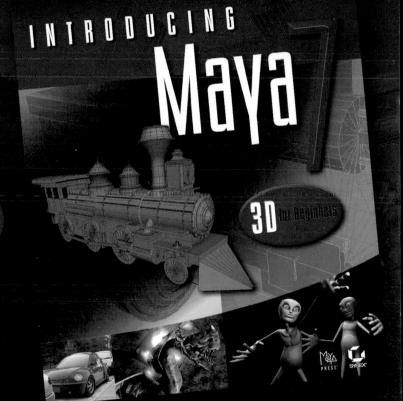